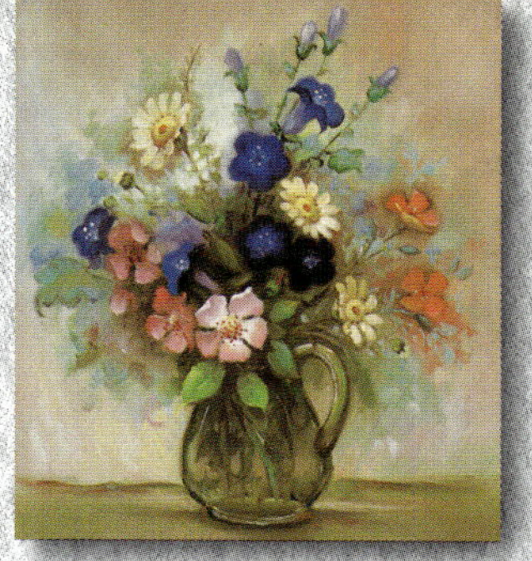

Floral Bouquets

Flowers are a timeless and enchanting subject, which is why they've long been a favorite subject of artists. From elegant roses to simple daisies, each has its own personality. Some flowers are mysterious, some are soothing, and some explode with excitement and drama. And when you group flowers together in a bouquet, the result is an array of rich colors and textures that makes a visually exciting and interesting still-life composition. With oil, you can paint thinly or thickly, so mimicking delicate flower petals and smooth surfaces is as easy as duplicating textured cloth or foliage. And the slow drying time of this medium makes it possible for you to fix mistakes as you work. With this book, you'll learn to produce beautiful, vibrant images in oil, creating florals that can be appreciated for a lifetime.

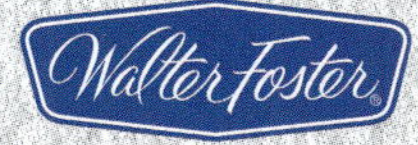

Gathering Your Supplies

Because there is a wide variety of items to choose from in art supply stores, it's easy to want one of everything! You really only need a few materials to begin your work. The golden rule is to buy the best products you can afford. Your purchase is an investment—if you take proper care of your brushes, paints, and palette, they will last a long time, and your paintings will last for generations. The basic, essential items are described here. For more information, you can refer to *Oil Painting Materials and Their Uses* by William F. Powell in Walter Foster's Artist's Library series.

BUYING OIL PAINTS

There are several different grades of paint available, from students' grade to artists' grade. Artists' grade paints are more expensive, but they contain better-quality pigments and fewer additives. The colors are also more intense and will stay true longer.

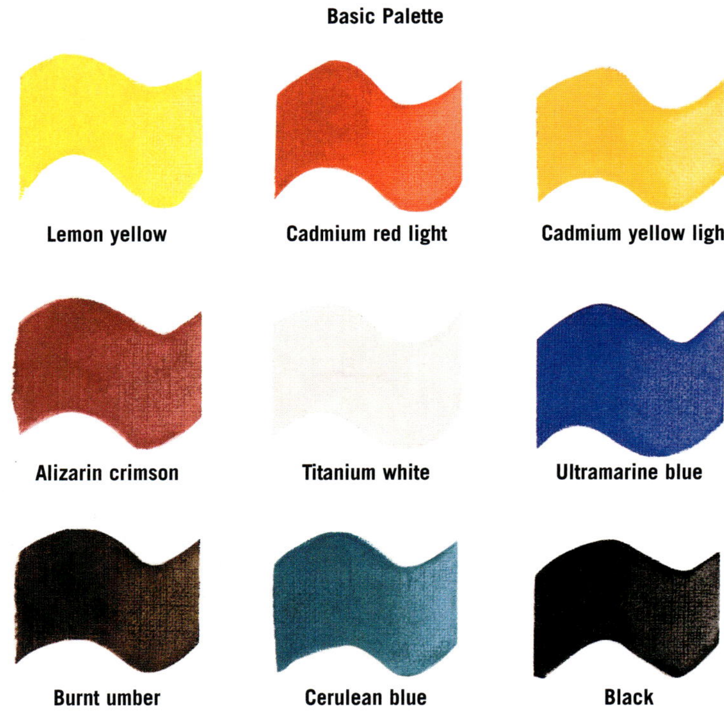

CHOOSING A PALETTE OF COLORS

A basic palette consists of the nine colors shown above (which includes a warm and a cool version of each of the primary colors). The artist featured in this book also has some unique colors in her palette. Hopefully her lessons will inspire you to try out some additional colors. Don't forget that there are many ways to mix a color—once you understand the basics of color theory, you can experiment with mixing a variety of colors. The more you practice, the easier it will seem! (For more on color, please see pages 4–5.)

Adding to the Palette

For the lessons described in this book, you'll need to supplement one or more of the colors listed below to your basic palette. (Refer to each project for color specifics.)

- ❑ cadmium red deep
- ❑ cadmium red medium
- ❑ rose red
- ❑ burnt sienna
- ❑ cadmium orange
- ❑ yellow ochre
- ❑ cadmium yellow medium
- ❑ sap green
- ❑ viridian green
- ❑ cobalt blue
- ❑ violet deep

SELECTING SUPPORTS

The surface on which you paint is called the "support," which is usually canvas or wood. You can stretch canvas yourself, but it's simpler to purchase prestretched, preprimed canvas (stapled to a frame) or canvas board (canvas glued to cardboard). If you're working with wood or other porous material, apply a primer first to seal the surface so the oil paints will adhere to the support (rather than soaking through).

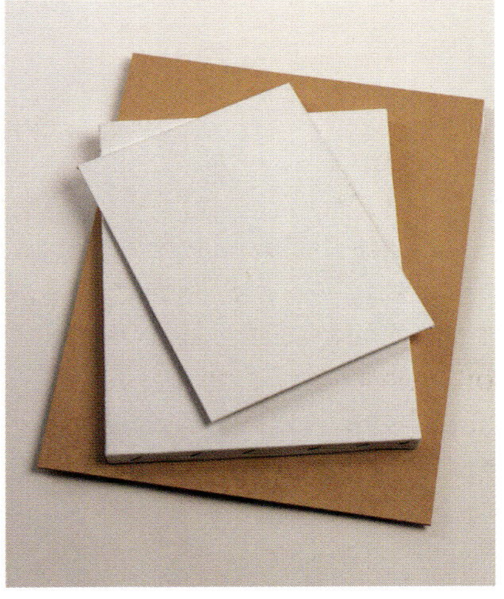

FINDING THE RIGHT SIZE Most stretched canvases, canvas boards, and wood boards are available in standard sizes. If you want to customize them, you can stretch your own canvases or cut down wooden boards to the exact sizes you require.

PURCHASING AND CARING FOR BRUSHES

There are many types of oil painting brushes available. There is no universal standard for brush sizes, so they vary slightly among manufacturers. Some brushes are sized by number, and others are sized by inches or fractions of inches. It is best to get brushes that are appropriate for the size of your paintings and are comfortable to work with. Brushes are also categorized by the material of their bristles; natural-hair brushes are generally regarded as the best for oil painting. The six brushes pictured below are a good starting set; additional brushes can be purchased later. Cleaning and caring for your brushes is essential—rinse them out well with turpentine and store them bristle side up or flat (never bristle side down).

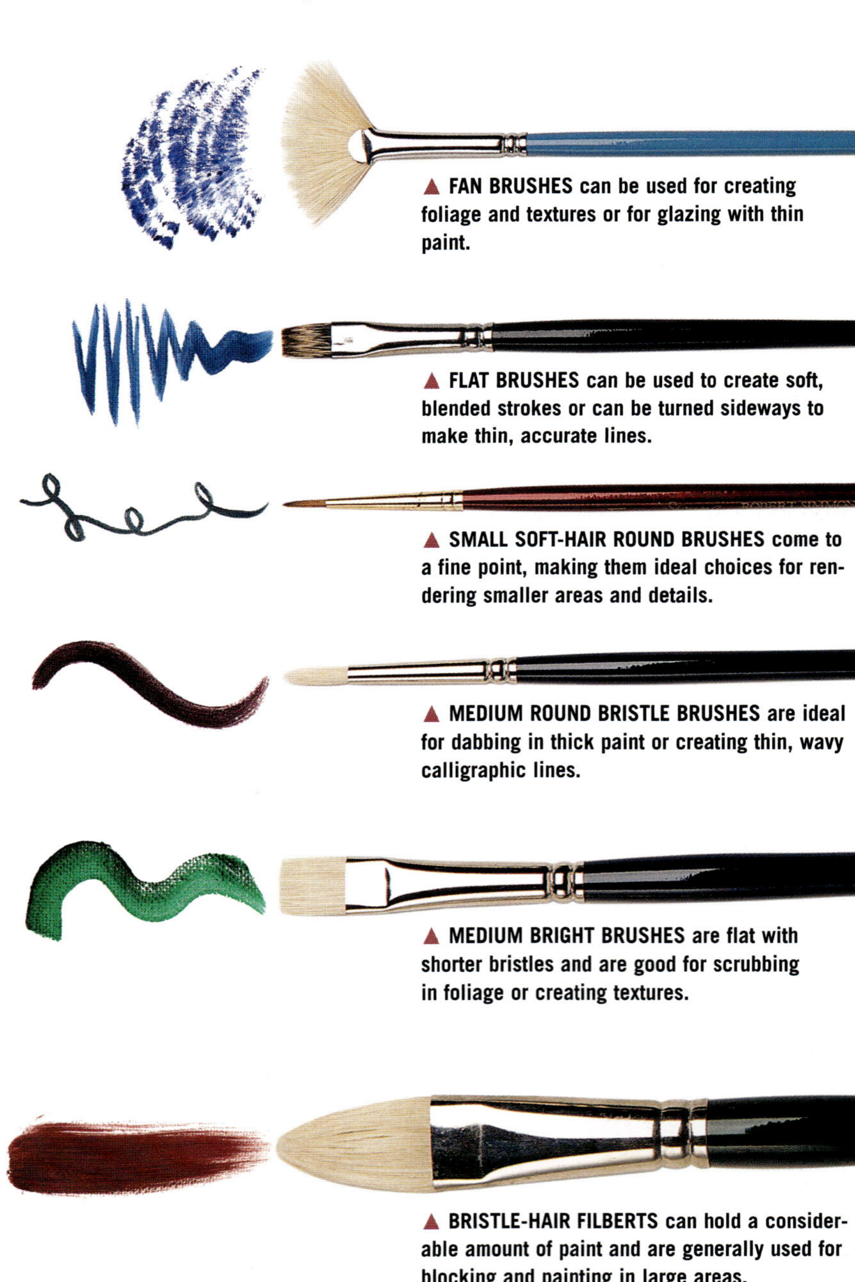

▲ **FAN BRUSHES** can be used for creating foliage and textures or for glazing with thin paint.

▲ **FLAT BRUSHES** can be used to create soft, blended strokes or can be turned sideways to make thin, accurate lines.

▲ **SMALL SOFT-HAIR ROUND BRUSHES** come to a fine point, making them ideal choices for rendering smaller areas and details.

▲ **MEDIUM ROUND BRISTLE BRUSHES** are ideal for dabbing in thick paint or creating thin, wavy calligraphic lines.

▲ **MEDIUM BRIGHT BRUSHES** are flat with shorter bristles and are good for scrubbing in foliage or creating textures.

▲ **BRISTLE-HAIR FILBERTS** can hold a considerable amount of paint and are generally used for blocking and painting in large areas.

USING ADDITIVES

Mediums and thinners are used to modify the consistency of paint. Many different types of oil painting mediums are available—some thin the consistency of the paint (linseed oil) and others increase drying time (copal). Others alter the finish or texture of the paint. Some artists mix a little turpentine with their medium to thin the color. You'll want to purchase some type of oil medium, since you'll need something to moisten the paint when it gets dries and to thin it for glazing and underpaintings. For cleaning brushes and for initial washes or underpainting, turpentine or mineral spirits can be used, but they aren't recommended as mediums. They break down the paint, whereas mediums actually help preserve the paint.

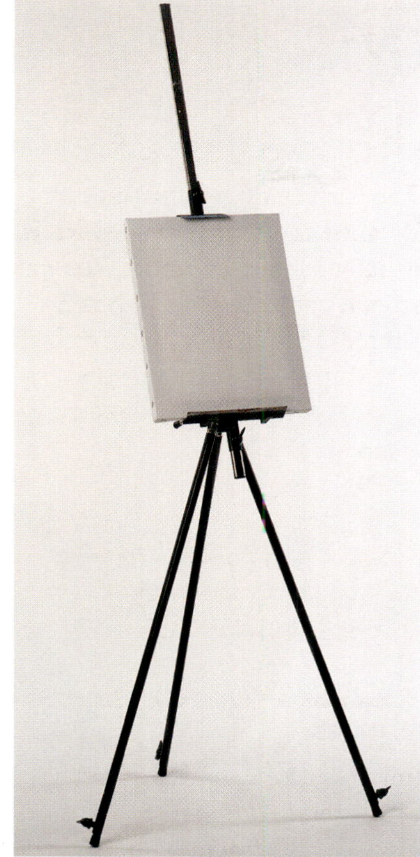

SELECTING AN EASEL The easel you choose will depend on where you plan to begin your composition. You can purchase a studio or tabletop easel for painting indoors, or you can buy a portable easel for outdoor sessions in informal settings.

Checklist of Basics

Below is a list of the materials you'll need to begin painting in oils. (For specifics, refer to the suggested brushes and colors on page 2.)

- ❑ 9 basic oil colors
- ❑ 6 brushes
- ❑ Medium (copal or linseed oil)
- ❑ Thinner (mineral spirits or turpentine)
- ❑ Palette and palette paper
- ❑ Containers for thinner and medium
- ❑ Palette knife
- ❑ Easel
- ❑ Supports
- ❑ Paper towels

PICKING A PALETTE

No matter what type of mixing palette you choose—glass, wood, plastic, or paper—make sure it's easy to clean and large enough to mix colors. Glass is a great surface for mixing paints and it is very durable. Palette paper is disposable, so cleanup is easy. And you can always purchase an airtight plastic box (or paint seal) to keep leftover paint fresh between painting sessions.

INCLUDING THE EXTRAS

Paper towels or lint-free rags are invaluable when oil painting; they can be used to clean tools and brushes or as creative tools to scrub in washes or soften edges. Some type of paint box is also useful to hold all your materials. In addition, pencils or charcoal are handy for sketching, and a mahlstick will help you steady your hand when working on a large support.

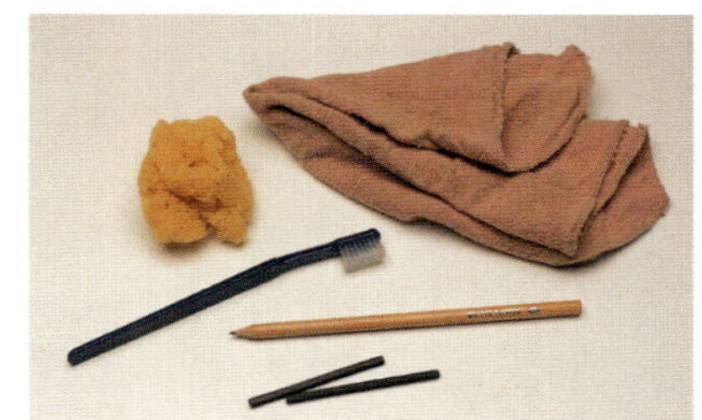

GATHERING EXTRAS In addition to the basic tools, you may also want to acquire a silk sea sponge and an old toothbrush for rendering special effects. Even though you may not use these additional items for every oil painting you work on, it's a good idea to keep them on hand in case you need them.

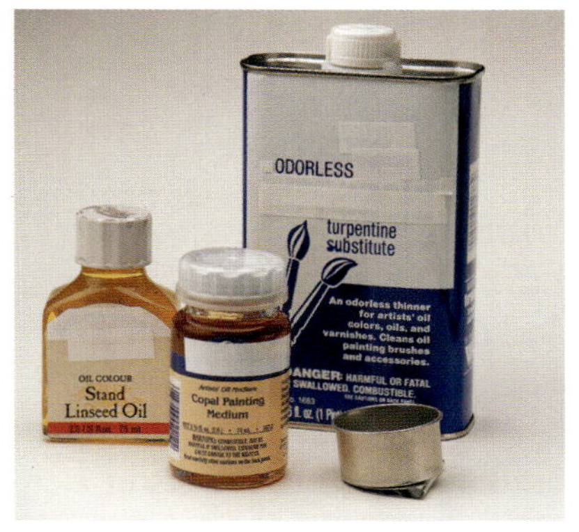

HOLDING MEDIUMS In addition to the chosen thinner or medium, be sure to purchase glass or metal containers—additives can be easily spilled and ruin your hard work! Some containers have a clip on the bottom to attach it to your mixing palette.

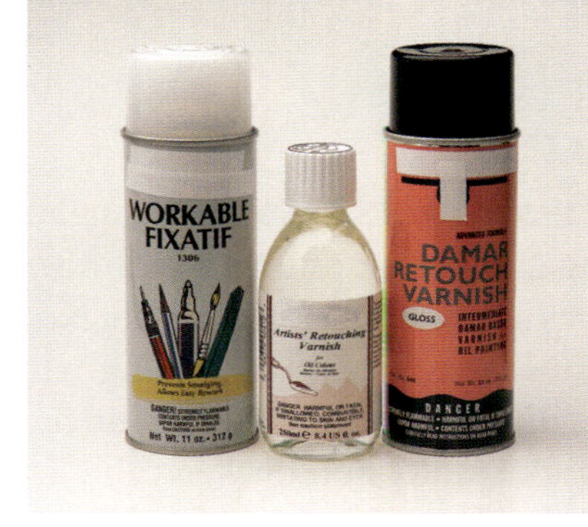

FINISHING UP Varnishes are used to protect a painting—spray-on varnish temporarily sets the paint, and brush-on varnish will permanently protect your work. Always read the manufacturer's instructions for application guidelines.

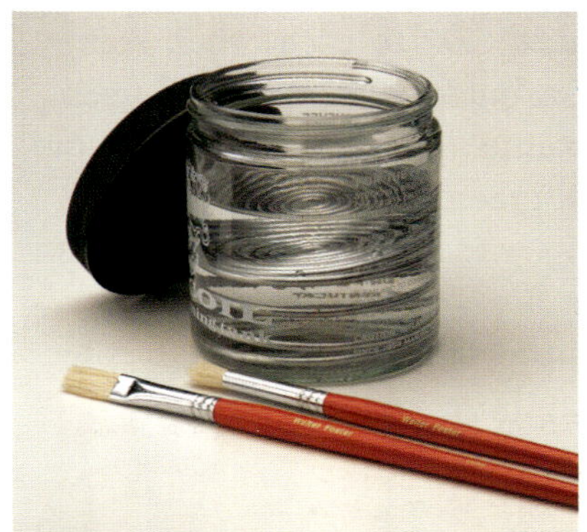

CLEANING BRUSHES A jar that contains a screen or coil can save some time and much mess. As the brush is rubbed against the coil, it loosens the paint and separates the sediment from the solvent. Once the paint has been removed, use brush soap and warm (never hot) water to remove any residual paint. Then reshape the bristles of the brush with your fingers and lay it out to dry.

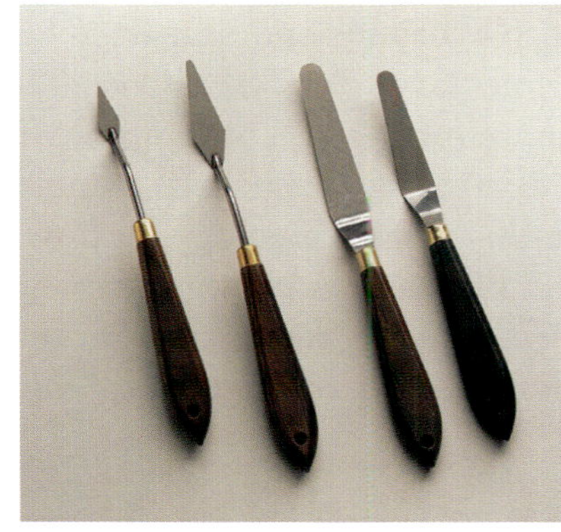

USING PAINTING AND PALETTE KNIVES Palette knives can be used either to mix paint on the palette or as tools for applying paint to a support. Painting knives usually have a small, diamond-shaped head, while palette (mixing) knives usually have a long, rectangular blade. Some knives have raised handles that help you avoid getting wet paint on your hand as you work.

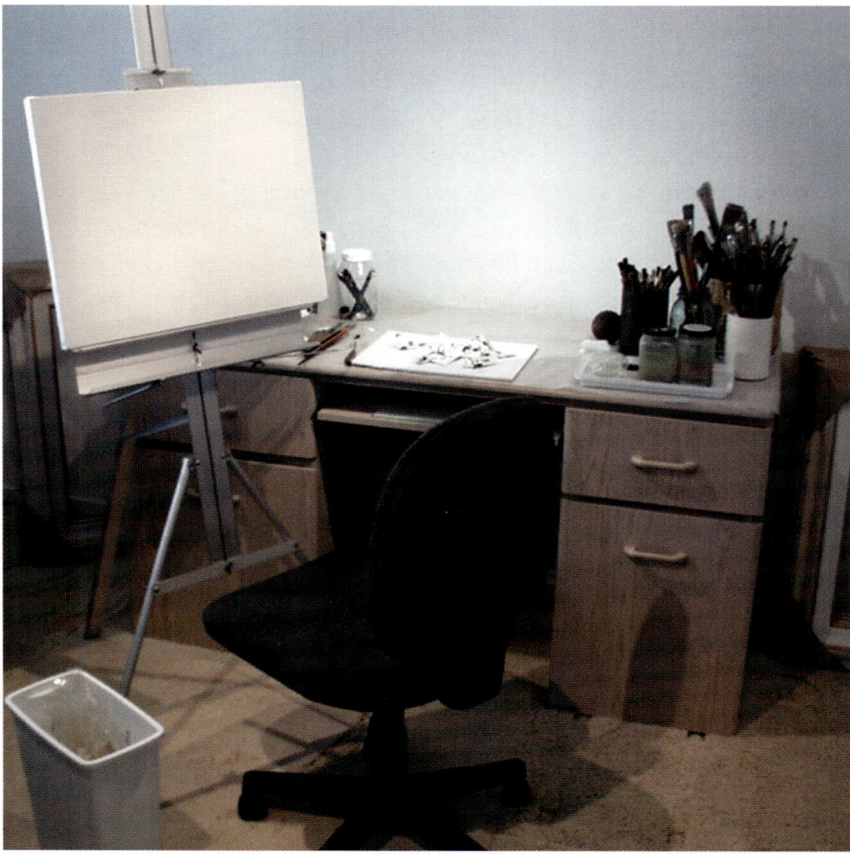

SETTING UP A WORK STATION How you set up your workspace will depend on whether you are right- or left-handed. It's a good idea to keep your supplies in the same place, so that each time you sit down to paint, you don't have to spend creative time searching for materials. If natural light is unavailable, make sure you have sufficient artificial lighting, and, above all else, make sure you're comfortable!

Applying Color Theory

A color wheel can be a handy visual reference for mixing colors. All the colors on the color wheel are derived from the three *primaries* (yellow, red, and blue). The *secondary* colors (purple, green, and orange) are each a combination of two primaries, and *tertiary* colors are mixtures of a primary and a secondary (red-orange, yellow-orange, yellow-green, blue-green, blue-purple, and red-purple). *Complementary* colors are any two colors directly opposite from each other on the color wheel, and *analogous* colors are any three colors adjacent on the color wheel. When considering color theory, there are several terms that are helpful to know. *Hue* refers to the color itself, such as red or yellow-green; *intensity* refers to a color's strength, from its pure state (right out of the tube) to one that is grayed or diluted; and *value* refers to the relative lightness or darkness of a color or of the combination of all colors: black.

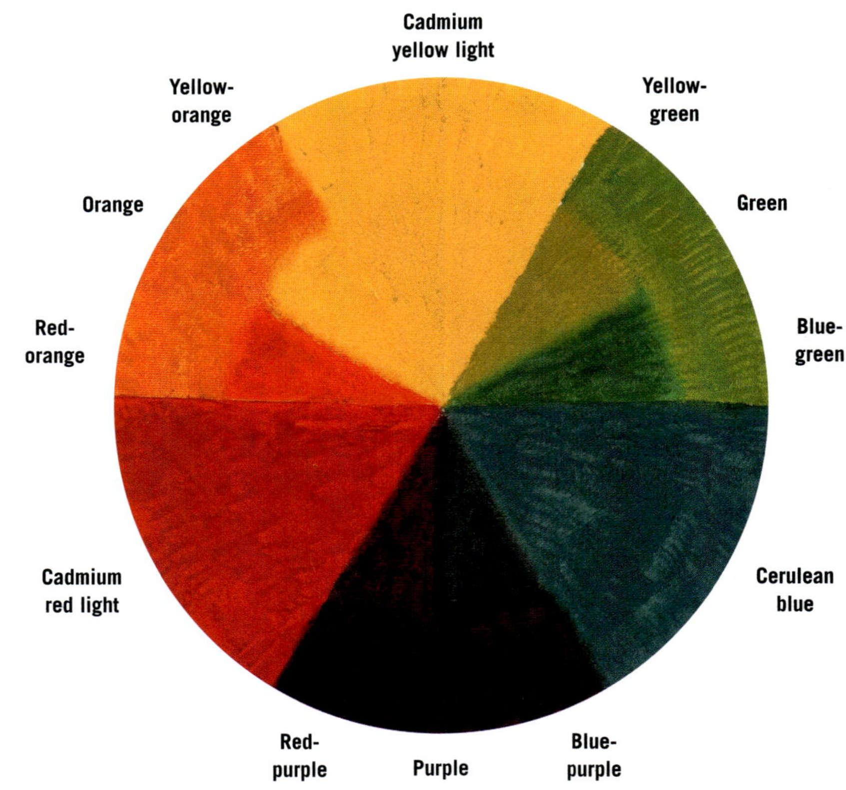

▲ **COLOR WHEEL** Knowing the fundamentals of how colors relate to and interact with one another will help you create a visual feeling—as well as interest and unity—in your oil paintings. You can mix just about every color from the three primaries. Primaries vary in temperature, however (see page 5 for more on temperature), so you'll eventually want to have at least two versions of each primary: one warm (containing more red) and one cool (containing more blue). These two primary sets will give you a wide range of secondary mixes.

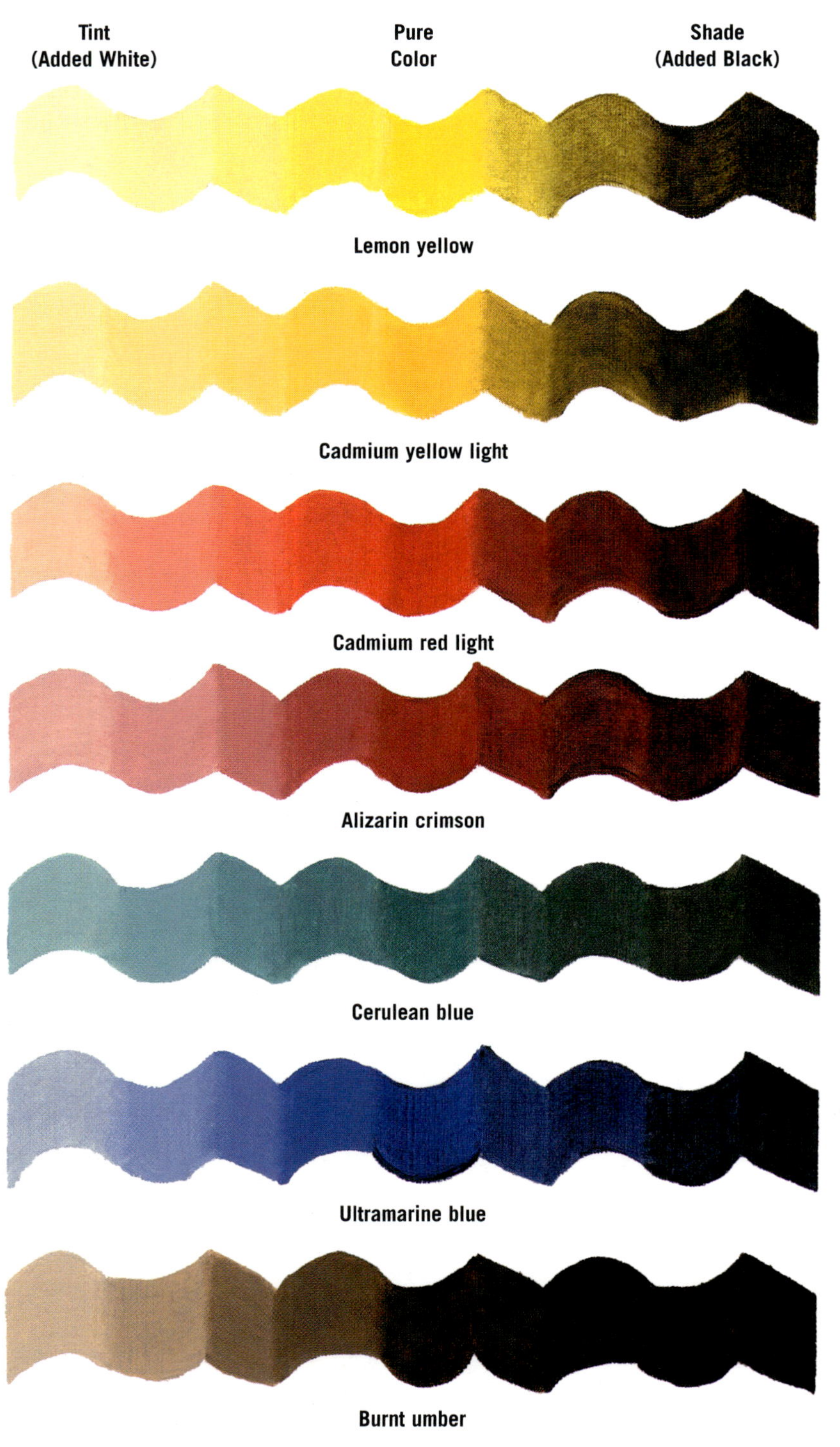

▲ **TINTS AND SHADES** The chart above shows varying tints and shades of different colors. The pure color is in the center of each example; the tints are to the left, and the shades are to the right.

VALUE

The variations in value throughout a painting are the keys to creating an illusion of depth and form. On the color wheel, yellow has the lightest value and purple has the darkest. You can change the value of any color by adding white or black (see the chart at left). Adding white to a pure color results in a lighter value *tint;* adding black results in a darker value *shade,* and adding gray results in a *tone.* (A painting done with tints, shades, and tones of only one color is called a "monochromatic" painting.) In any painting, the very lightest values are the highlights and the very darkest values are the shadows.

COMPLEMENTARY COLORS

As stated above, complements are any two colors directly opposite each other on the color wheel, such as red and green, yellow and purple, or blue and orange. When placed next to each other, complementary colors create visual interest, but when mixed, they neutralize (or "gray") one another. For example, to neutralize a bright red, mix in a touch of its complement: green. By mixing varying amounts of each color, you can create a wide range of neutral grays and browns. (In painting, mixing neutrals is preferable to using them straight from a tube because neutral mixtures provide fresher, more realistic colors that are more like those found in nature.)

▶ **DIRECT COMPLEMENTS** Each of these examples is a pair of direct complements. Direct complements create the most striking contrasts when placed next to one another. When you want to create more drama or vitality in your paintings, place a color next to its complement.

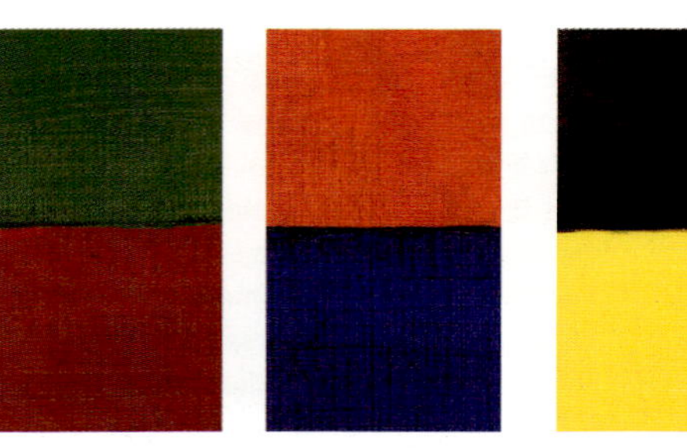

UNDERSTANDING COLOR PSYCHOLOGY

Colors on the red side of the color wheel are considered "warm," while colors on the blue side of the wheel are thought of as "cool." Warm colors can convey energy and excitement, whereas cool colors can evoke a calm, peaceful mood. Within all families of colors, there are both warm and cool hues. For example, a cool red (such as alizarin crimson) contains more blue, and a warm red (such as cadmium red) contains more yellow. Keep in mind that cool colors tend to recede, while warmer colors appear to "pop" forward. You can use the contrast between warm and cool colors to help portray a sense of distance or dimension in a composition.

MIXING COLOR

Successfully mixing colors is a learned skill, and, like anything else, the more you practice, the better you will become. One of the most important things is to train your eye to really see the shapes of color in an object—the varying hues, values, tints, tones, and shades of the subject. Once you can see them, you can practice mixing them. If you're a beginner, you might want to go outside and practice mixing some of the colors you see in nature at different times of day. Notice how the colors of things seem to change as the light changes; the ability to see the variations in color under different lighting conditions is one of the keys to successful color mixing.

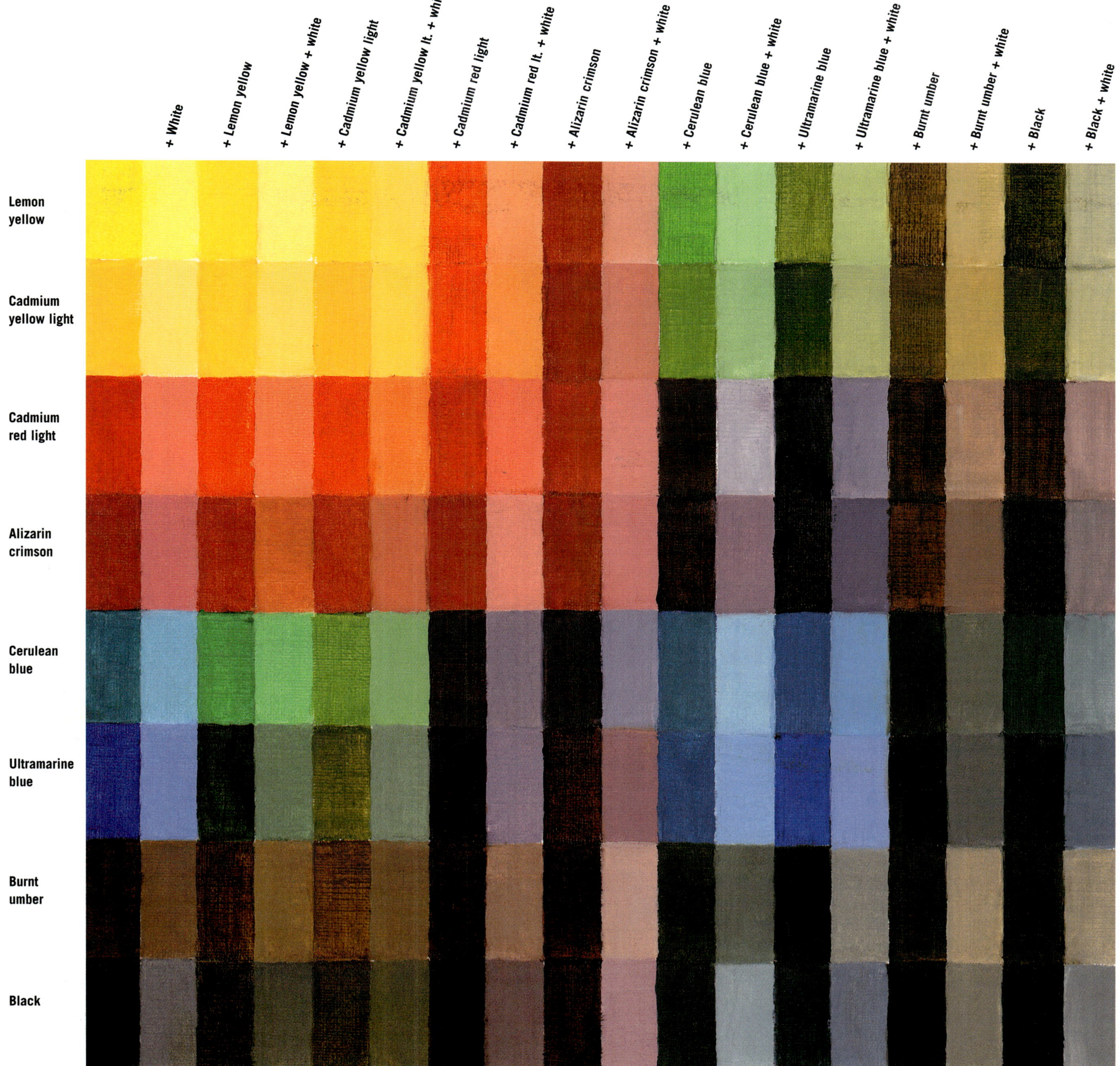

USING A LIMITED PALETTE You don't need to purchase dozens of tubes of paint to be able to mix a vast array of hues. Instead you can use a limited number of paints and mix the other colors you need. The chart above shows just some of the colors that can be made using the nine colors found in the basic palette listed on page 2. You may want to create your own chart using the colors from your palette; this is an excellent exercise in learning to mix color.

Basic Shapes

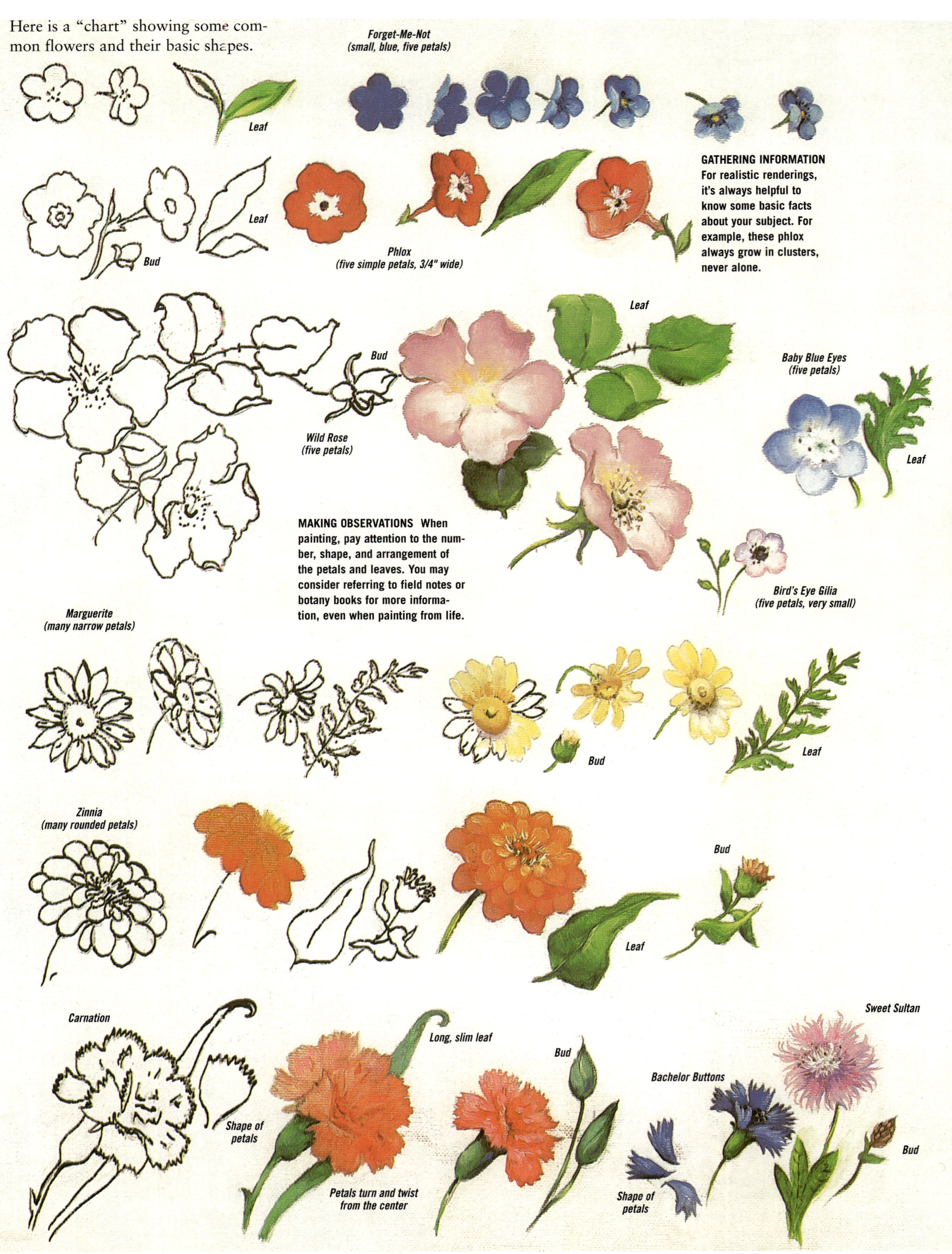

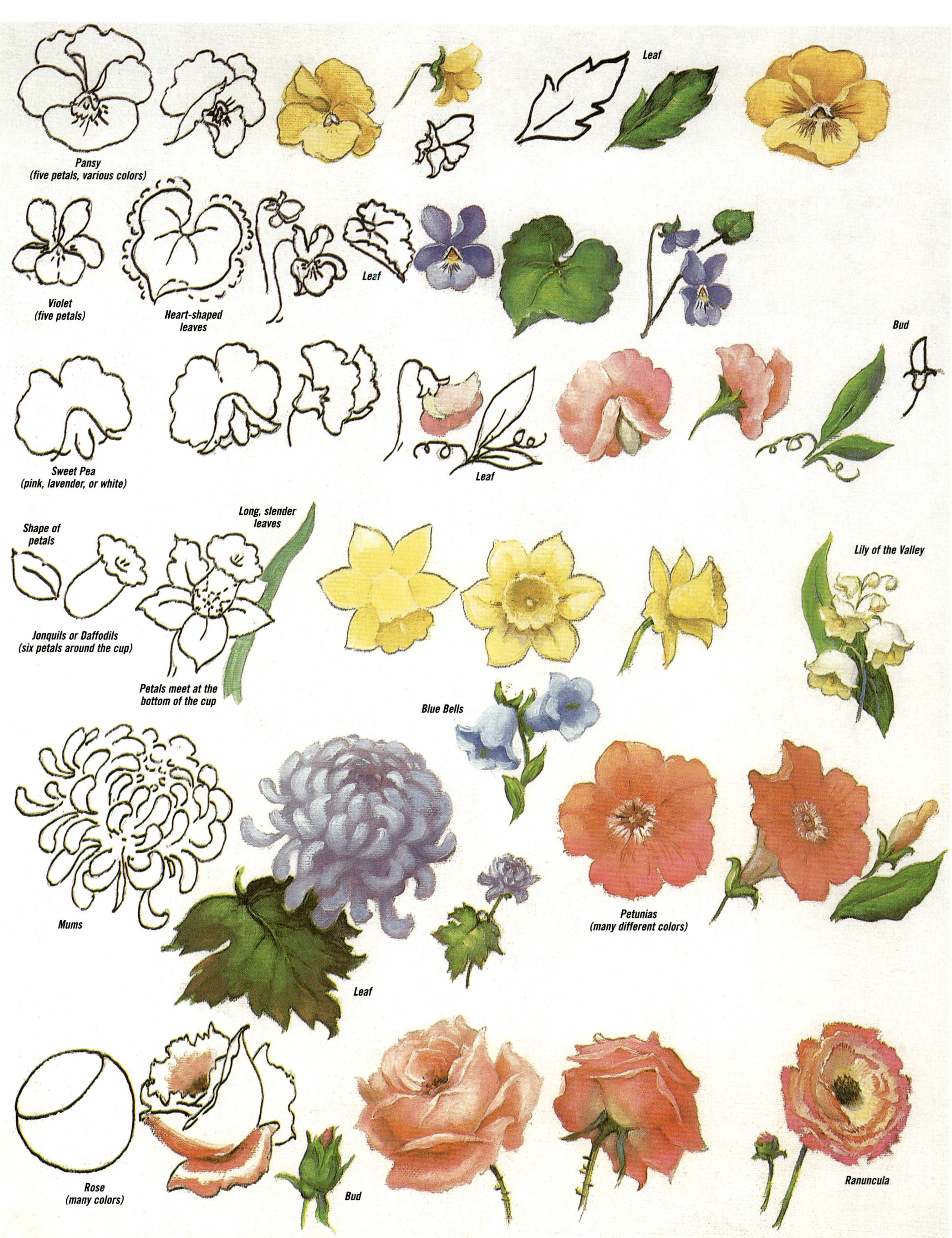
Leaf
Pansy
(five petals, various colors)
Violet
(five petals)
Heart-shaped
leaves
Leaf
Bud
Sweet Pea
(pink, lavender, or white)
Leaf
Shape of
petals
Long, slender
leaves
Lily of the Valley
Jonquils or Daffodils
(six petals around the cup)
Petals meet at the
bottom of the cup
Blue Bells
Mums
Petunias
(many different colors)
Leaf
Rose
(many colors)
Bud
Ranuncula

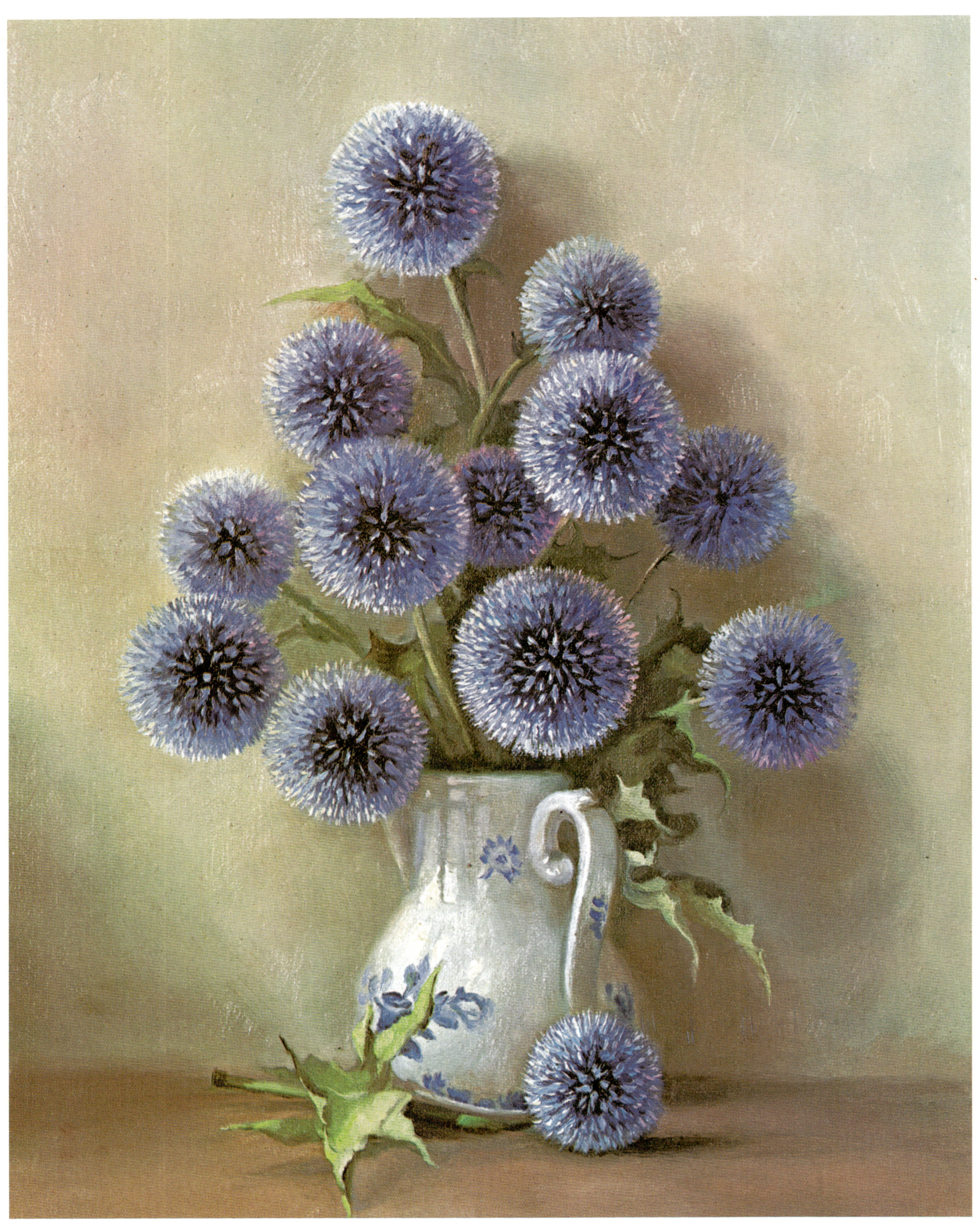

SETTING UP A STILL LIFE This beautiful arrangement of blue flowers has a strong composition for a floral still life. *Composition* refers to the relationships among the objects in a painting. And a good composition uses colors, shapes, and lines to lead the viewer's eye on a visual path into and around the painting, toward the *center of interest* (also referred to as the *focal point*). But a composition doesn't have to be complex to make a visual impact. The simple shapes of this arrangement are pleasing to the eye because the leaves, stems, and handle of the vase direct your eye to the focus: the bouquet. The strong highlights and shadows, the variation in the size of the flowers, and the distinction between the shape of the flowers, leaves, and vase all contribute to the painting's appeal.

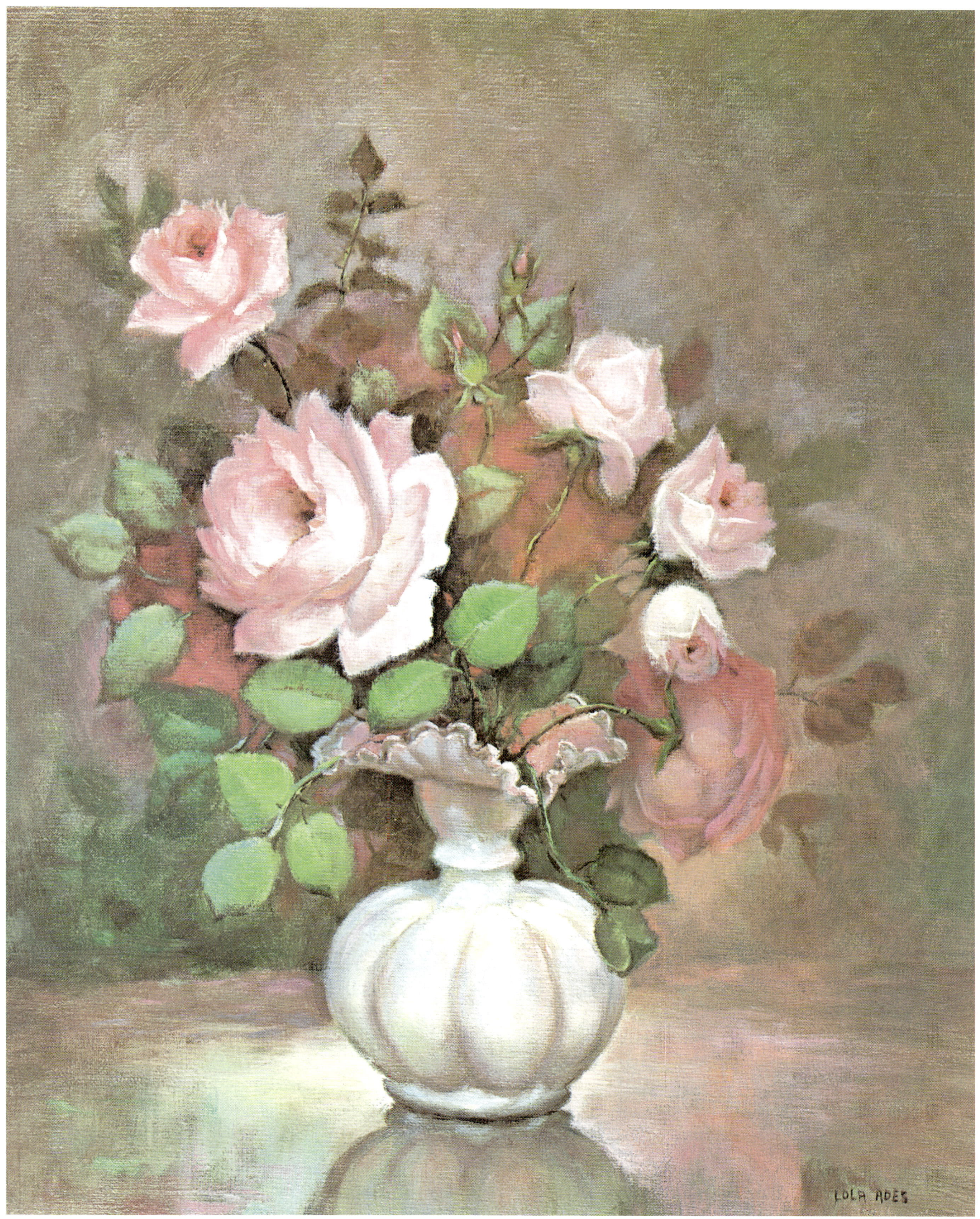

ADDING VARIATION No matter what the subject, variation is key to composing a dynamic painting. In this delicate rose arrangement, the flowers are hardly uniform; despite the similarities, each individual flower has a unique size and shape. And each bud, blossom, and stem is placed at a slightly different angle, all facing in varied directions. Notice also that the stems and leaves are flowing and bent, rather than straight or stiff, creating interest by producing an illusion of change and movement. Furthermore these roses aren't placed in an even, straight row, which would make the composition dull and boring. Instead overlapping flowers give depth to the painting; the flowers in front seem closer to the viewer, while the flowers behind appear to be farther away.

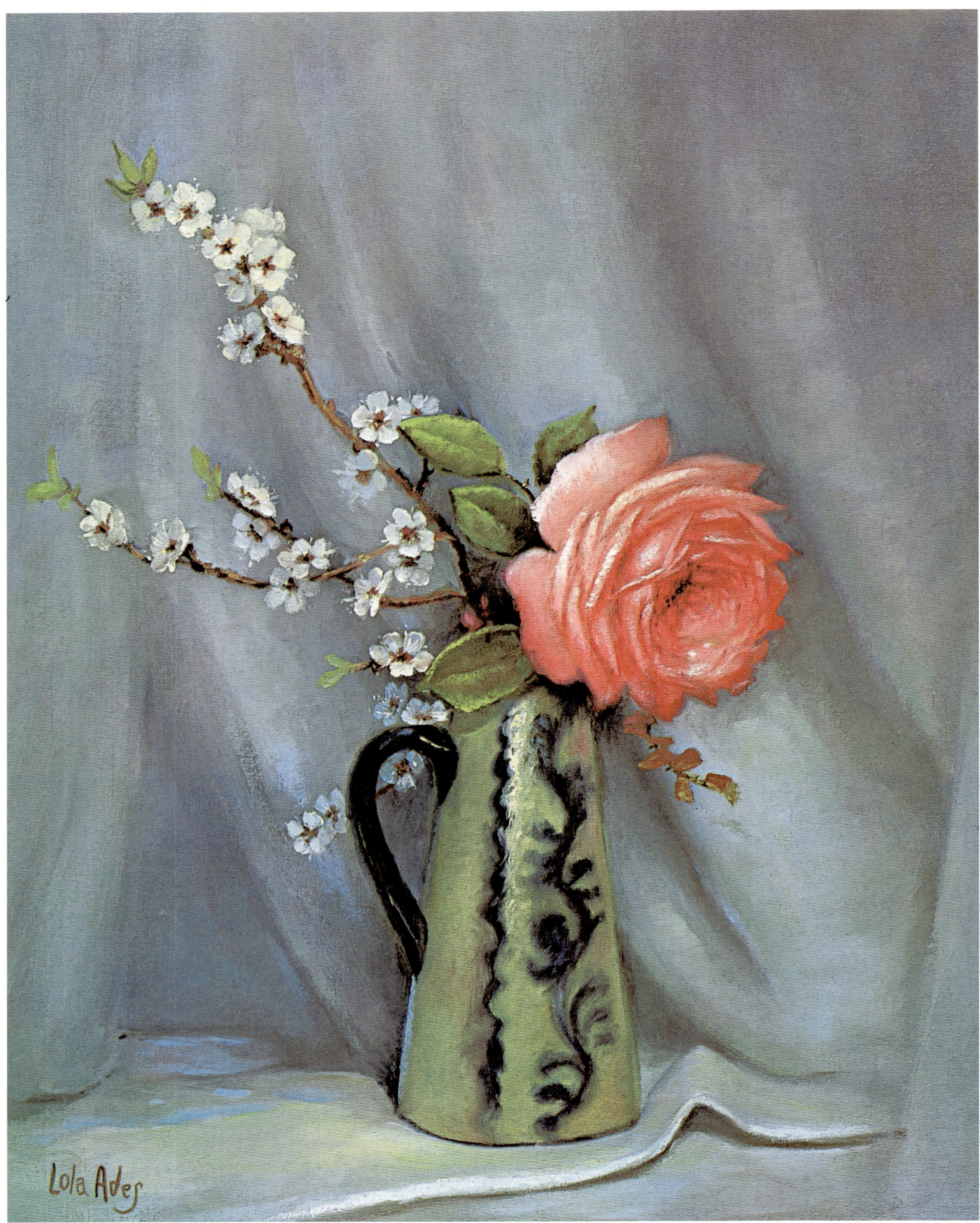

CONTROLLING LIGHT One way to add drama and interest to a painting is to manipulate the light source. The interplay between light and shadow can become a striking component of your composition. It's important to keep your light source in mind while painting, so that your highlights and shadows are consistent with its placement. In this simple bouquet, the light is coming from above left, creating warm highlights on the higher apricot blossoms. Where the blossoms are in shadow, they become cooler and more blue. Note the highlights on the handle of the pitcher and the reflection of the blue drape on the picture. Though plain, the drape is another essential element of this painting; its folds and wrinkles help direct the eye around the painting and toward the rose.

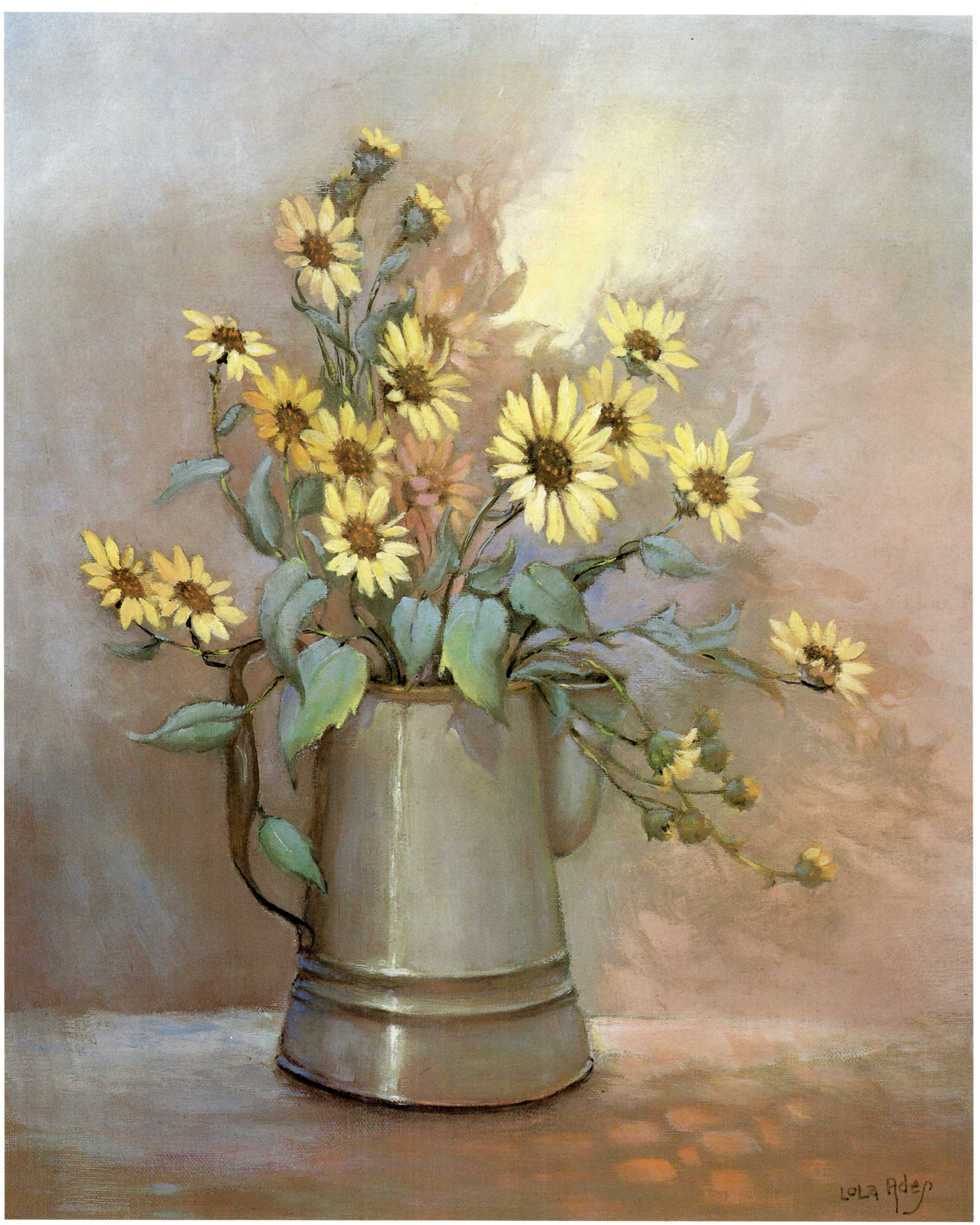

CHOOSING A CONTAINER Your choice of container is just as important as the flowers you select for your still life. Glass and metal vases have a hard, reflective sheen, and when these smooth, shiny shapes are paired with soft, textured flowers, it creates an intriguing contrast. Even dull metals have interesting highlights and reflections, so don't veer away from including these. And organic materials, including woven baskets or wooden crates, can imbue your painting with a more natural feeling. But don't limit yourself to tradition. A ceramic crock or a watering can be as effective as a glass pitcher or crystal vase, as you can see in this simple painting. And feel free to use your *artistic license* to change the color of your containers to create contrasts or harmonies.

PAINTING THE POT To paint the pot, first sketch your design on canvas. This pot has a round top, so you'll want to draw a rounded bottom as well (this same rule applies to any container with a round top, whether a pot, vase, or pitcher). Sketching an ellipse for the bottom of the container (below left) will help you to establish dimension before you begin painting. Now paint the pot with cadmium red light mixed with ultramarine blue, adding white to achieve the lighter values. As you paint, be sure to blend your edges (below right) so that they appear rounded (not as if they have sharp edges). To finish, "anchor" the container by painting a shadow underneath it.

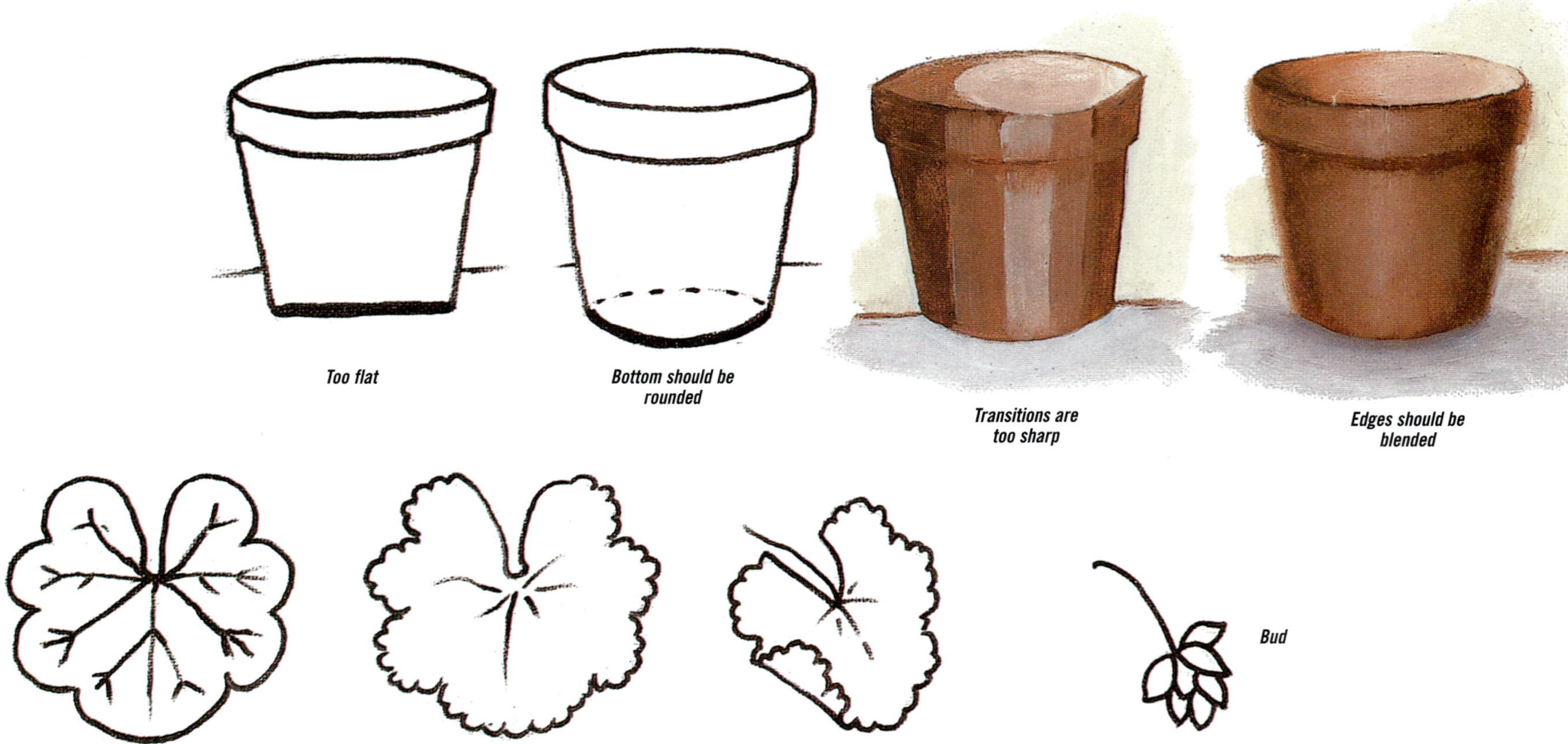

SUGGESTING LEAVES When you sketch the leaves, keep in mind that the leaves toward the front require the most detail, but you'll still want to simplify the vein patterns so that they don't draw too much attention away from the focus of the flowers. And don't worry about duplicating the rounded, scalloped edges of the geranium leaves exactly; it's enough to suggest their general shape and angle. As you work toward the back of the plant, simplify the leaves even more. Then paint the leaves of the geranium with zinc lemon yellow mixed with ultramarine blue. To enhance the sense of dimension, dull the leaves in the background with a touch of cadmium red light.

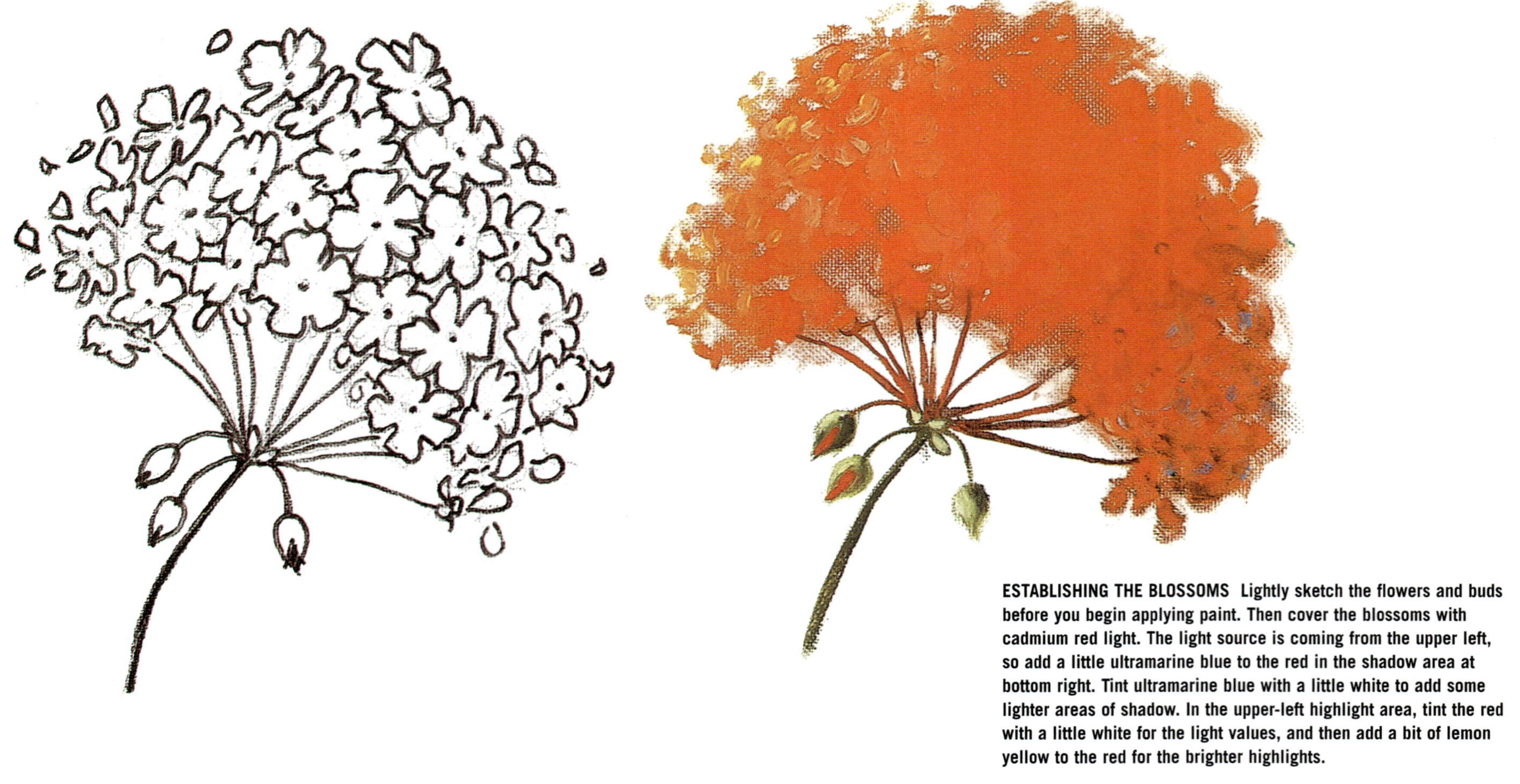

ESTABLISHING THE BLOSSOMS Lightly sketch the flowers and buds before you begin applying paint. Then cover the blossoms with cadmium red light. The light source is coming from the upper left, so add a little ultramarine blue to the red in the shadow area at bottom right. Tint ultramarine blue with a little white to add some lighter areas of shadow. In the upper-left highlight area, tint the red with a little white for the light values, and then add a bit of lemon yellow to the red for the brighter highlights.

Separating the elements of your composition and dealing with them individually can help simplify the painting process for beginners. Here the basic elements of the painting on page 13 have been broken out and demonstrated individually to help clarify how each is painted. This painting also uses a very limited palette of warm versions of the three primary colors: ultramarine blue, cadmium red light, and zinc lemon yellow. As you can see, you don't need to buy a huge assortment of colors to create beautiful bouquet paintings. You can mix almost any color you can imagine from the just the basic primaries and a little white paint!

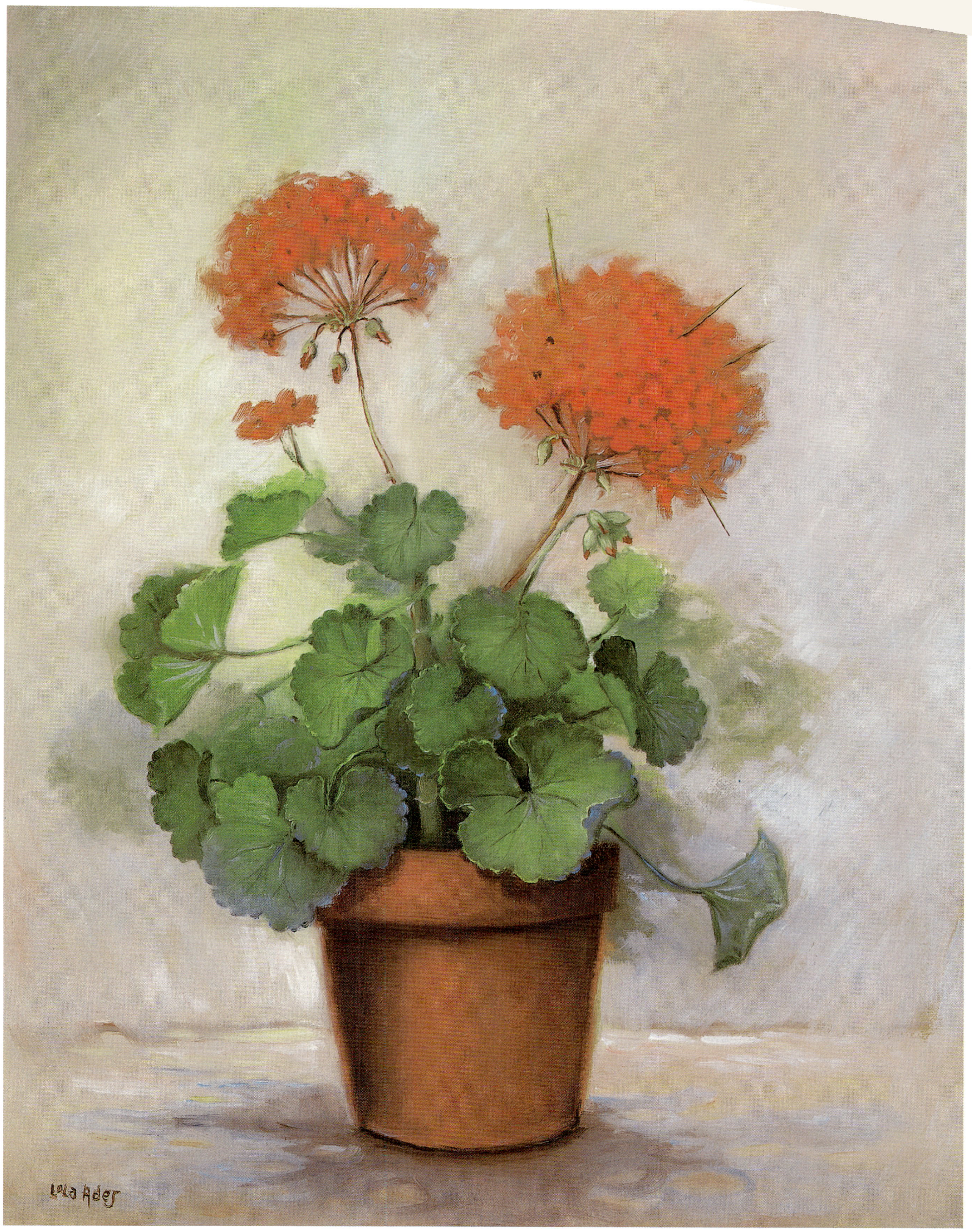

Once you have painted the pot, the flowers, and the leaves, paint the stems using the same color mixes used for the leaves and flowers. Then create a range of neutrals for the background by mixing each color with a bit of its complement; the color opposite it on the color wheel (such as red and green, purple and yellow, or orange and blue). Use more yellow in the upper-left corner and more red on the right, adding more or less white so you have a range of values. Paint the background right up to and even overlapping the blossoms, leaves, and stems a bit. This will keep them from looking like cardboard cutouts against the table and background.

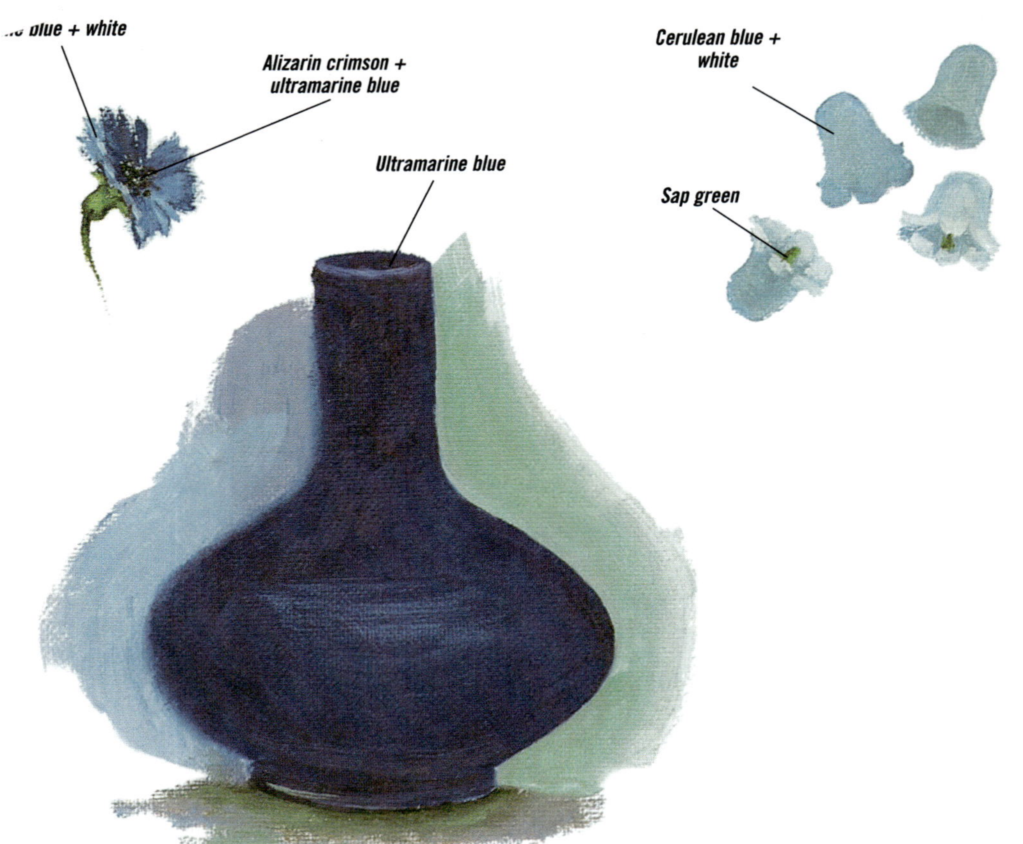

SOFTENING EDGES Blend the edges of the vase (shown above left) and the flowers into the background to make them look three-dimensional. Sharp, clean edges (shown above right) make the object look flat and "pasted on."

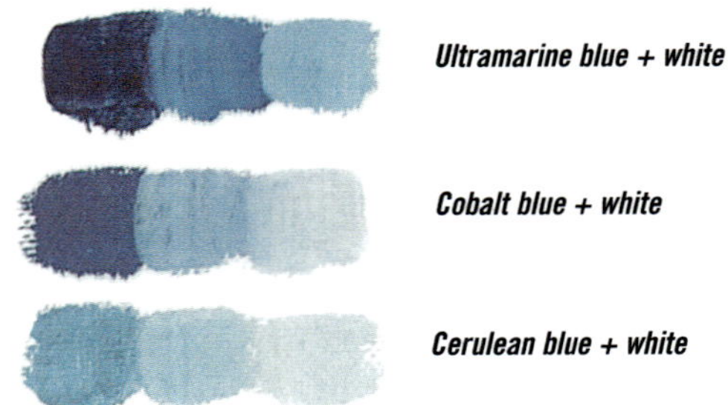

DISTINGUISHING BLUES Though all blues are in the same family of color, there can be a lot of difference between them. Ultramarine blue is a deep, rich blue; cobalt blue is a more medium color; and cerulean blue has a cool, greenish quality to its hue.

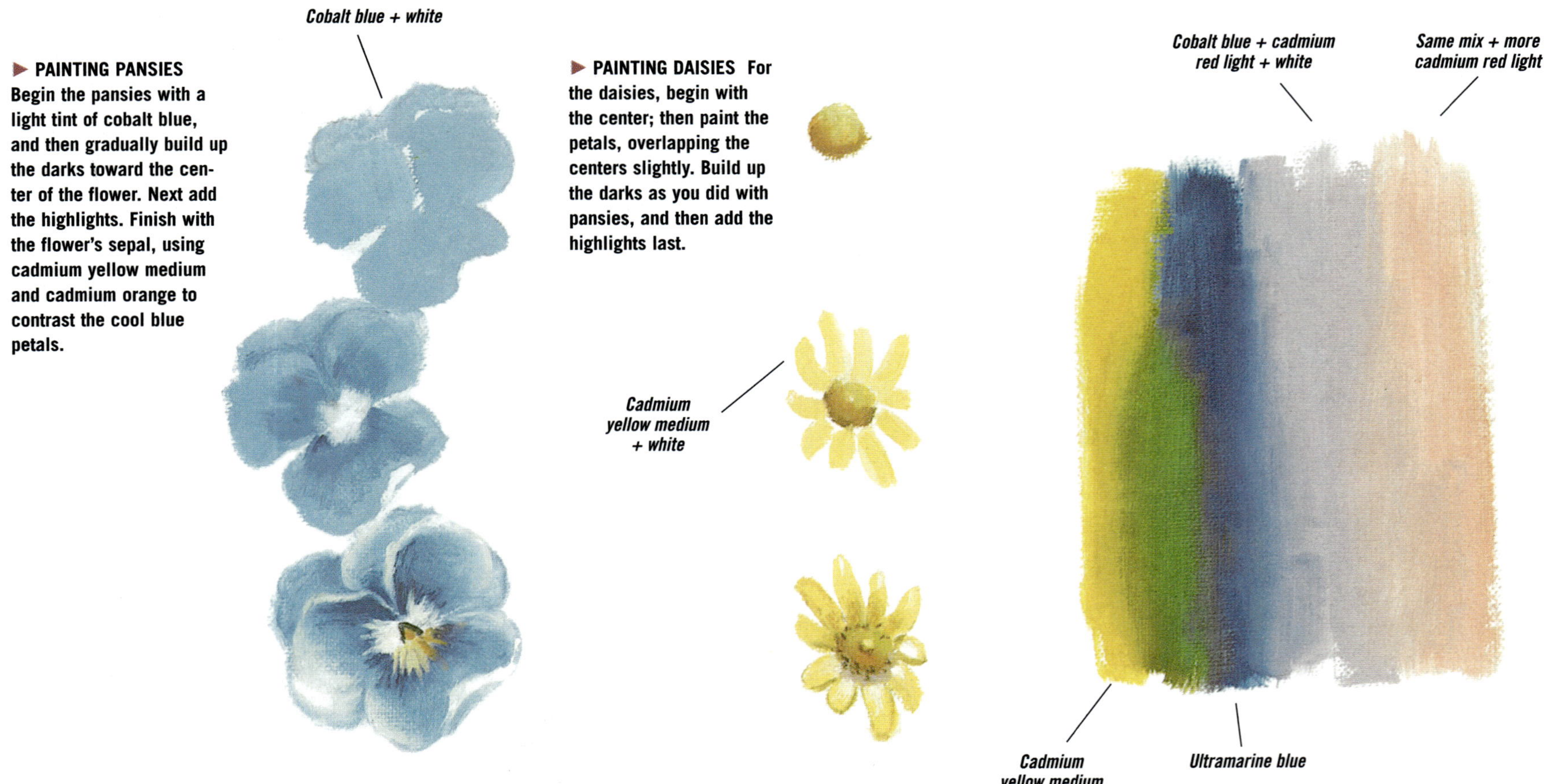

► **PAINTING PANSIES** Begin the pansies with a light tint of cobalt blue, and then gradually build up the darks toward the center of the flower. Next add the highlights. Finish with the flower's sepal, using cadmium yellow medium and cadmium orange to contrast the cool blue petals.

► **PAINTING DAISIES** For the daisies, begin with the center; then paint the petals, overlapping the centers slightly. Build up the darks as you did with pansies, and then add the highlights last.

A good color scheme doesn't have to be a complicated one. By restricting your palette to one color (monochromatic) or just a few—such as blue, yellow, and green—you can create a very striking piece. This painting uses a *limited palette,* composed mostly of blues (ultramarine, cobalt, and cerulean), but it also makes use of white, viridian green, cadmium yellow, lemon yellow, and even a few neutralizing reds. To paint this peaceful bouquet, concentrate on one aspect of the composition at a time, beginning with the vase; then develop the flowers and establish the background. Remember to keep blending all your edges as you paint!

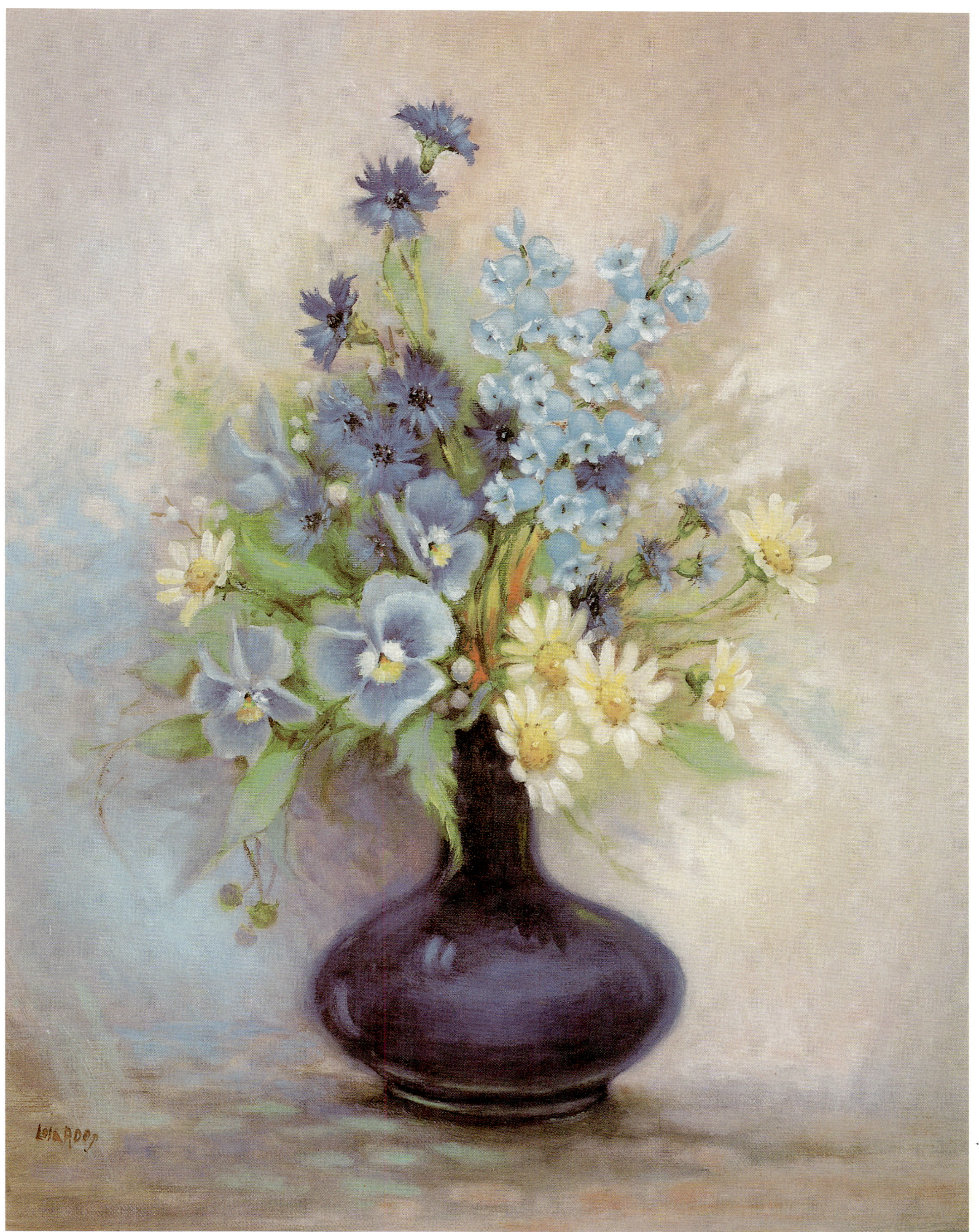

Look over your painting as you go along. If you find something that isn't quite right, study, think, and try to remedy it. The beauty of oil paints is that they dry so slowly. You can always scrape away areas you don't like and paint over them, "fixing" mistakes. Notice the way the colors of the bouquet, such as the leaf mixture of viridian green, white, and lemon yellow, are repeated in the background to create a sense of color harmony. Orange and red, the complements of blue and green, are also used for accents; these hints of warmer colors are enough to create interest but not so bright as to overpower the subject.

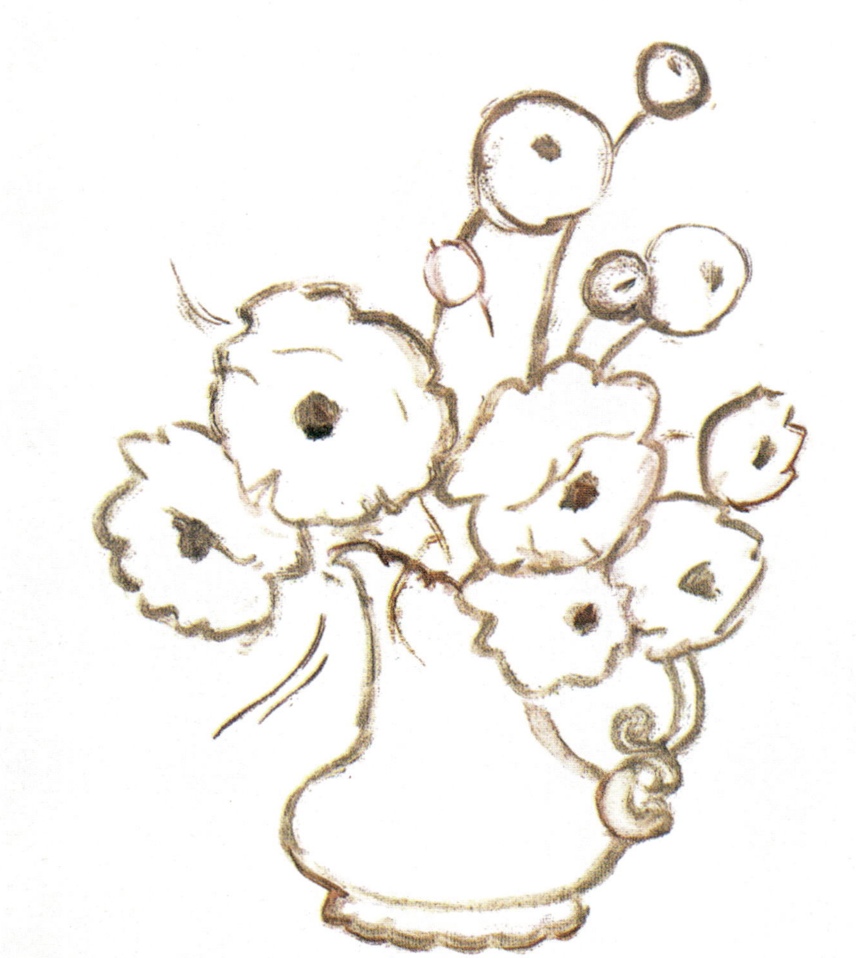

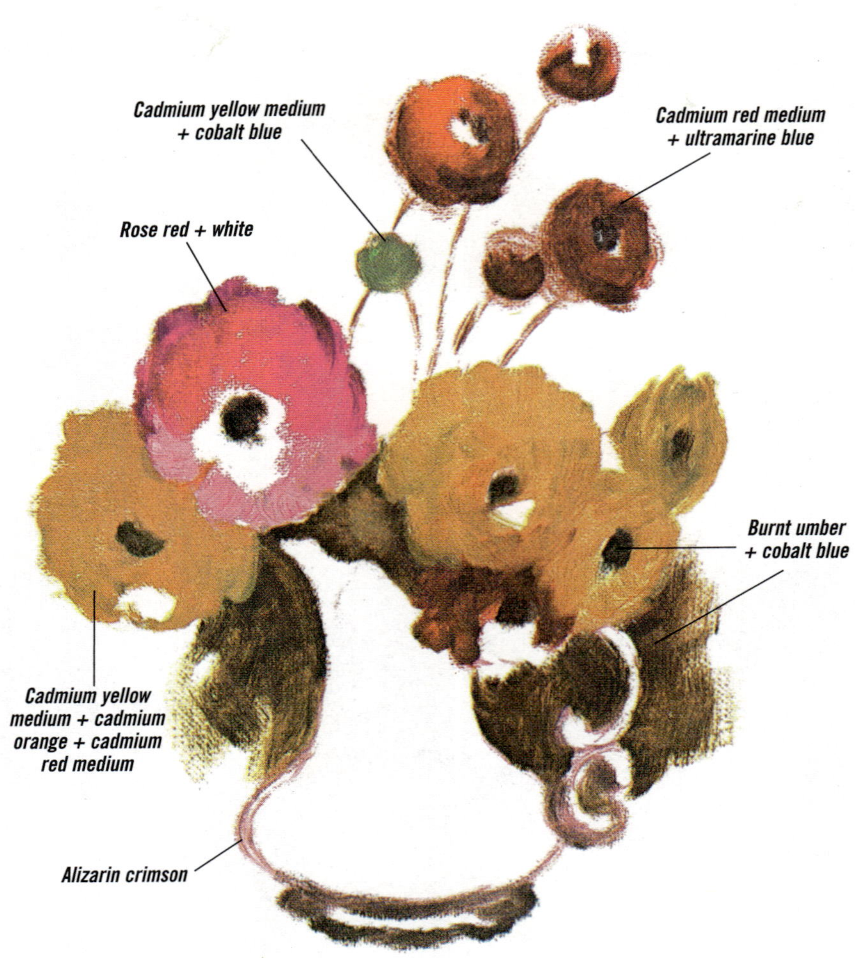

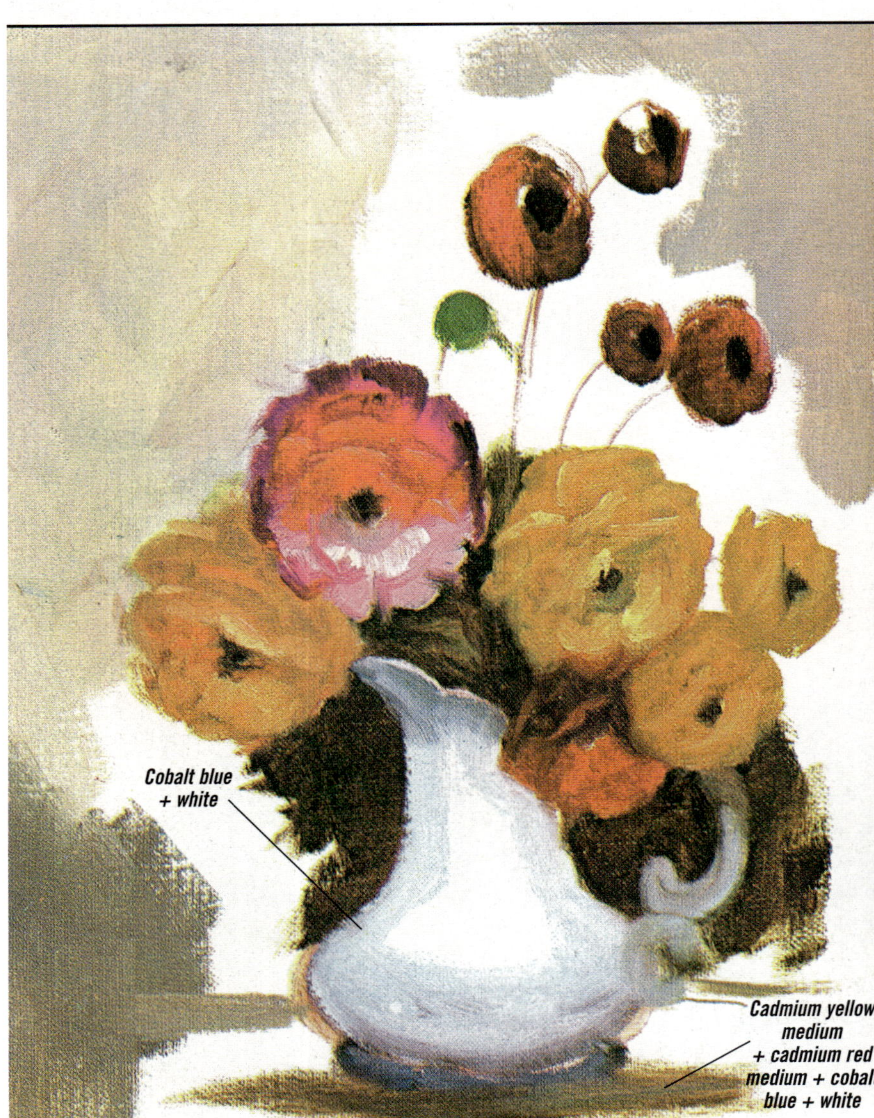

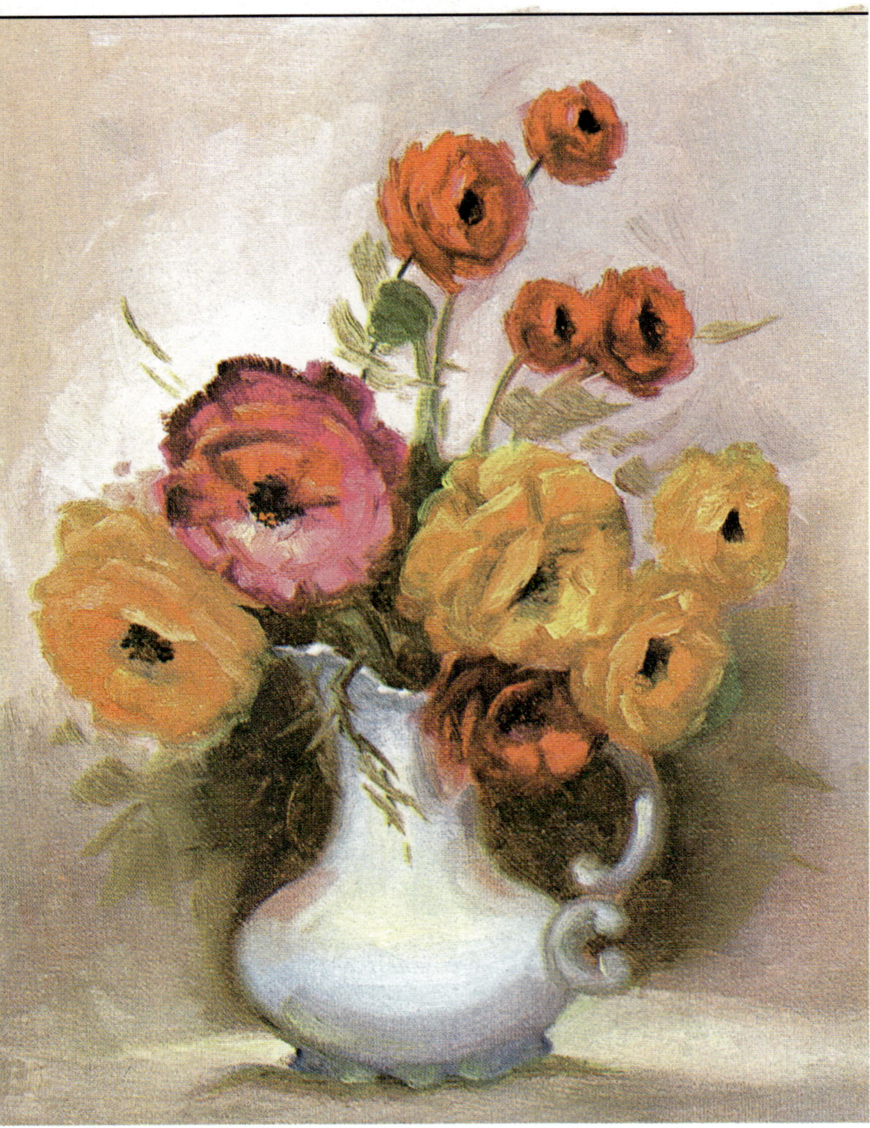

The intense green background complements the vibrant flowers in this bouquet. To begin, sketch the basic shapes with a thin, neutral mix, using alizarin crimson in the warmer areas, such as at the base of the vase. Then block in the dark values of the flowers. Paint the exterior background with a light, neutral color. Then block in the pitcher starting with white, adding cobalt blue in the shadows and cadmium yellow medium in warmer spots. Continue building up the darks. Then add the greenery and increase the intensity of the background green using cadmium yellow medium mixed with cobalt blue. Next add highlights and shadows on the flowers and pitcher.

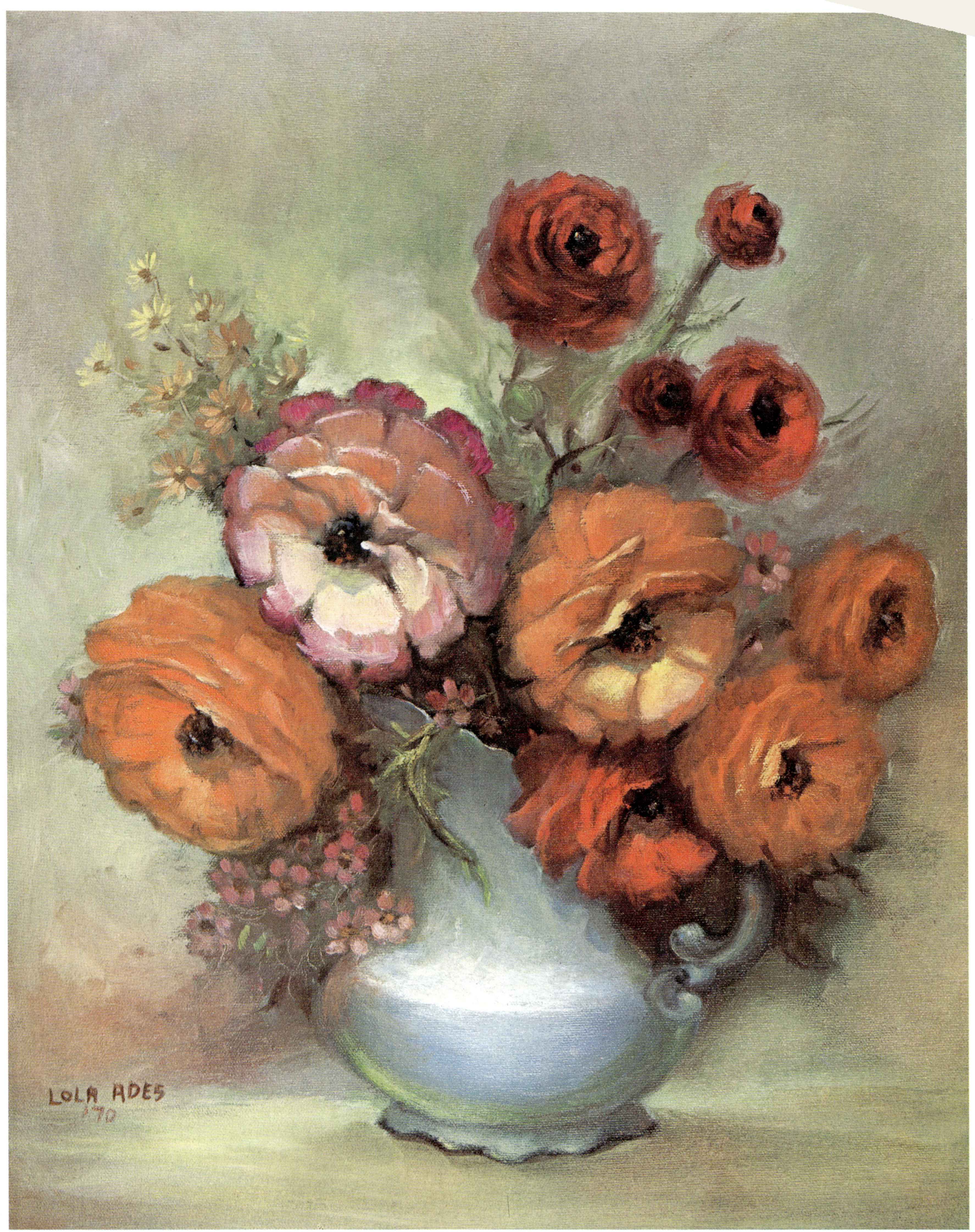

Now refine the painting by building up your final layers of color, paying careful attention to placing the highlights and shadows according to the light source. Build up the background colors with warmer greens, grays, and a few pinks. Be sure that your blends are soft and even, especially on the rounded edges (such as the bowl of the pitcher and along the edges of the flower petals). Add some groups of tiny flowers in more muted tones to balance out the large, colorful ranunculas in the bouquet. As you finish the white pitcher, keep in mind that its surface reflects the surrounding colors—from the green surface its sitting on to the adjacent red blossoms.

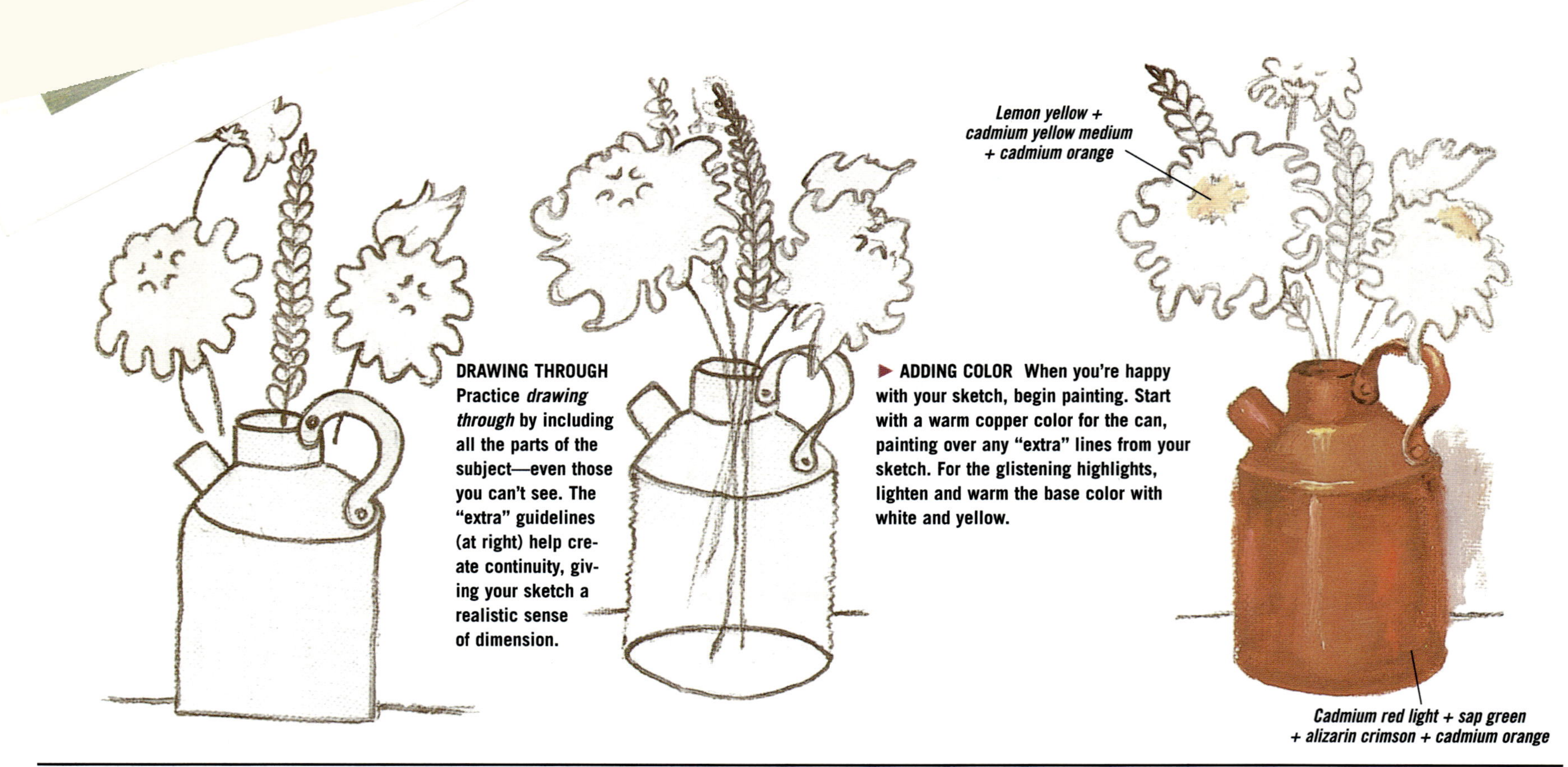

DRAWING THROUGH Practice *drawing through* by including all the parts of the subject—even those you can't see. The "extra" guidelines (at right) help create continuity, giving your sketch a realistic sense of dimension.

► **ADDING COLOR** When you're happy with your sketch, begin painting. Start with a warm copper color for the can, painting over any "extra" lines from your sketch. For the glistening highlights, lighten and warm the base color with white and yellow.

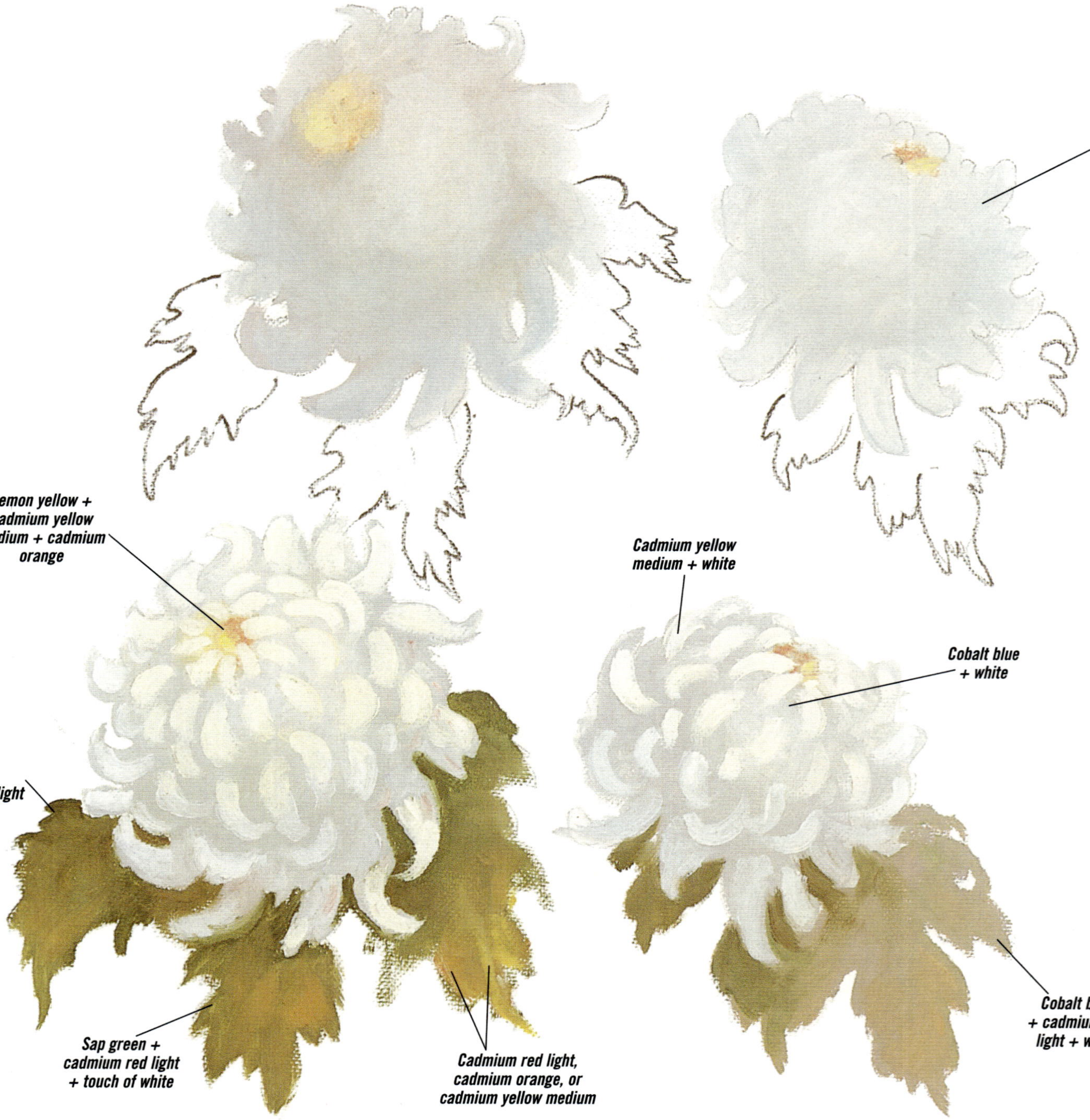

Viridian green + alizarin crimson + white

Lemon yellow + cadmium yellow medium + cadmium orange

Cadmium yellow medium + white

Cobalt blue + white

Sap green + cadmium red light

Sap green + cadmium red light + touch of white

Cadmium red light, cadmium orange, or cadmium yellow medium

Cobalt blue + cadmium red light + white

This painting takes a slightly untraditional approach by mixing neutral gray tones in with the leafy greens; these grays enhance the shadowy white colors of the mums. To begin painting, cover the mum petals with a light gray base coat. Then, with quick swipes of the brush, paint the petal highlights and shadows. On the forefront leaves, use darker browns and greens toward the blossom, lightening with warm red, orange, and yellow highlights at the tips. Keep the leaves in the background and in shadow largely gray.

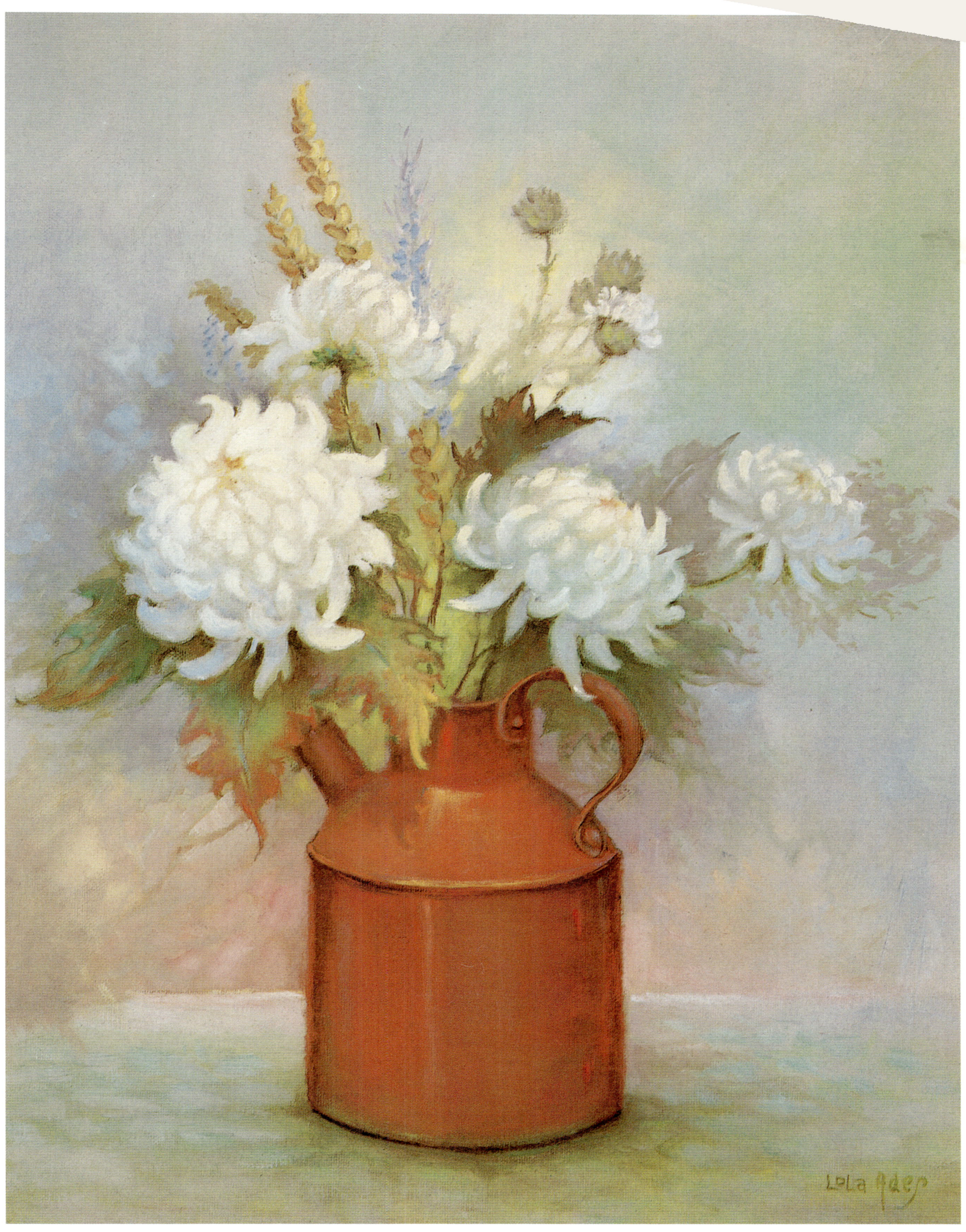

Now paint a few extra sprigs and flowers for accents. You don't want these to draw too much attention, so keep them cool in tone, but use the same palette of colors to create harmony in your painting. For the background, begin at the top with viridian green mixed with white; then work in cobalt blue at the left. The bright green is a mix of lemon yellow, viridian green, and white. For the warm shades near the can, mix alizarin crimson and white (for the pinks) and cobalt blue, alizarin crimson, and white (for the violet).

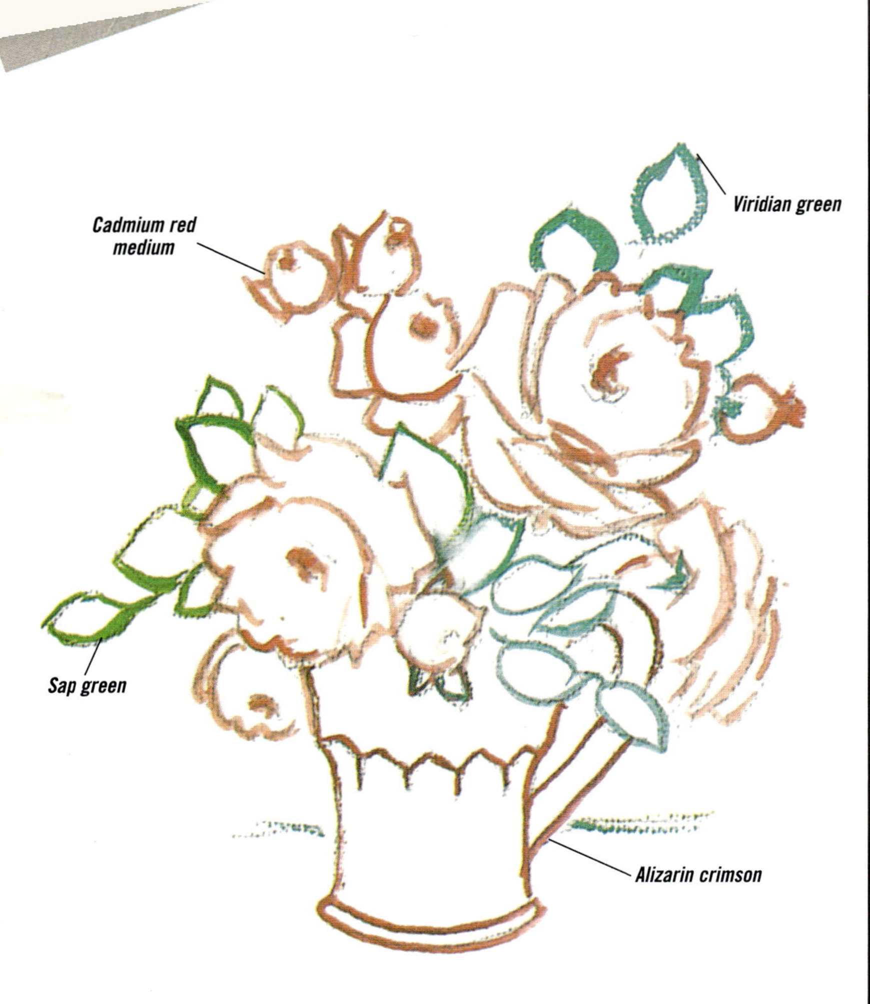

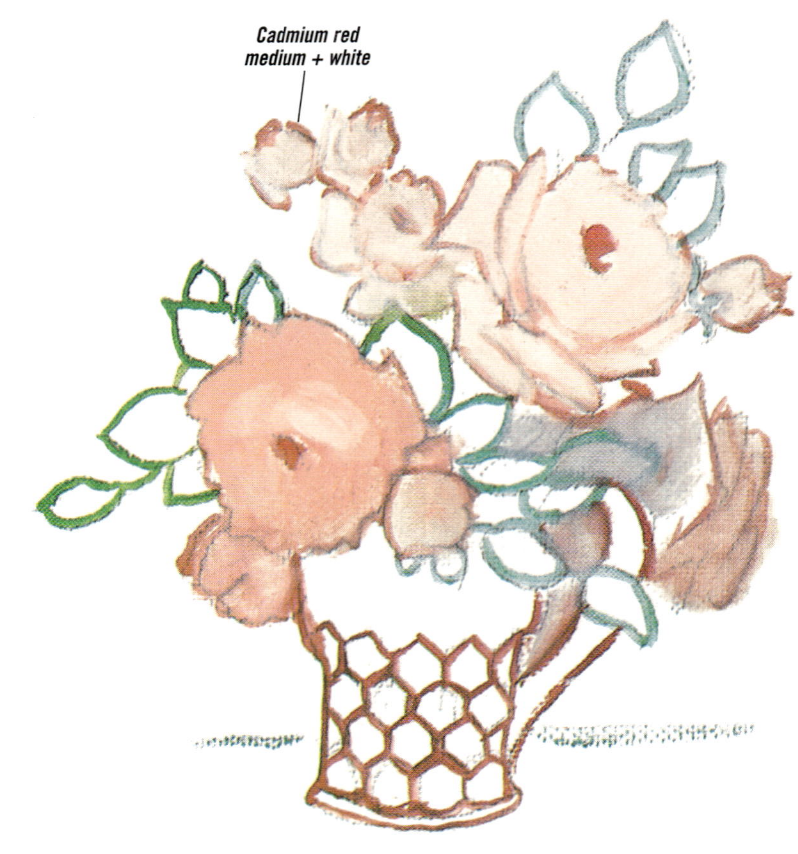

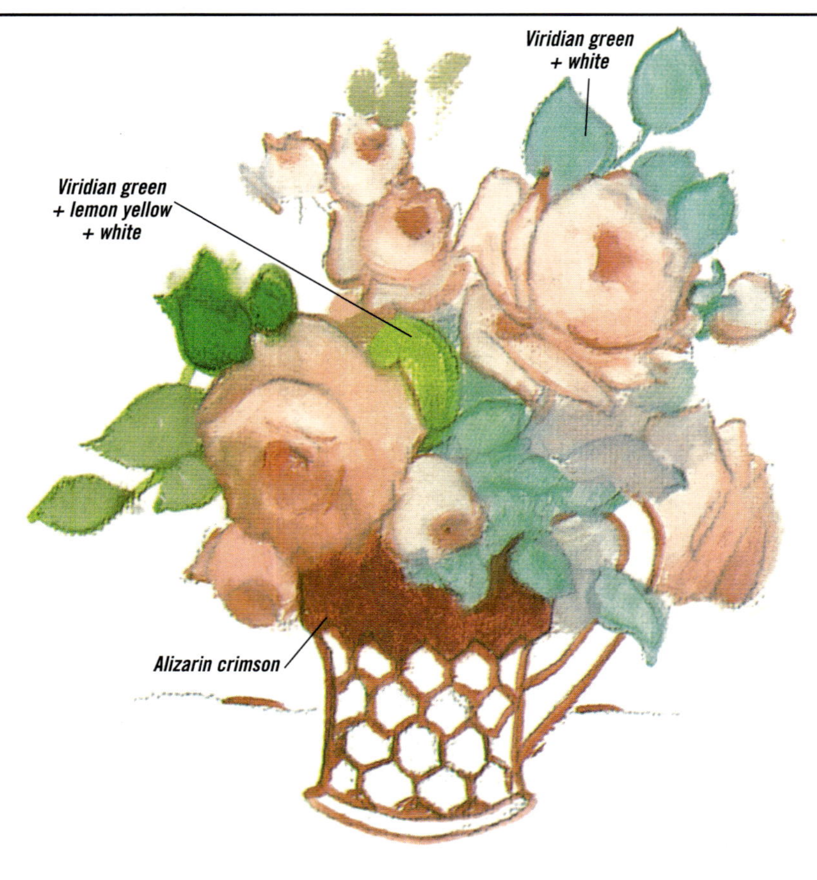

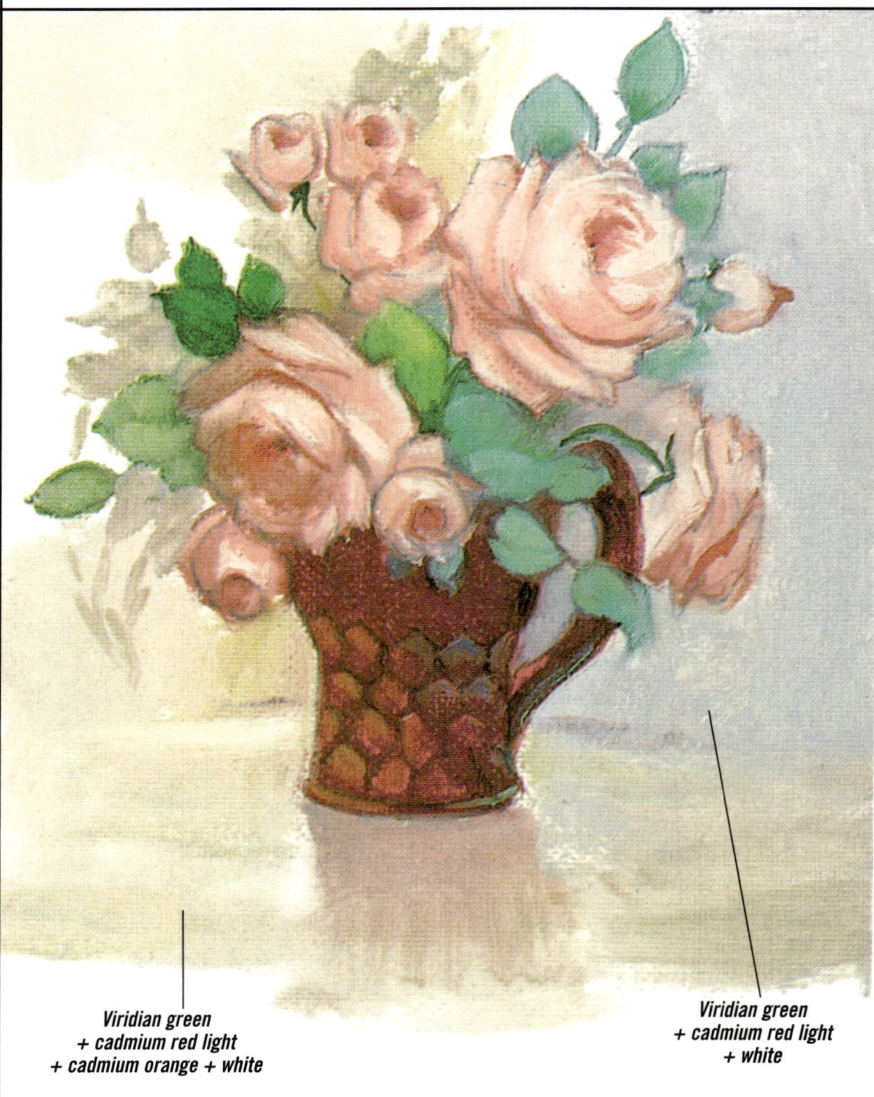

These cabbage roses have analogous colors that create a harmonious composition. Alizarin crimson, cadmium red medium, and cadmium red light are all reds, but they vary from cool to warm, which keeps the painting from becoming too monotonous. Sketch in your basic shapes to start, and then begin filling in the blossoms with varied tints of cadmium red medium. To accent the roses, use both warms and cools within the greenery as well; then fill in the glass pitcher with alizarin crimson. For the highlights on the pitcher, use cadmium orange, another color analogous to the reds. Work in the background last, making it cooler in the shadows at right.

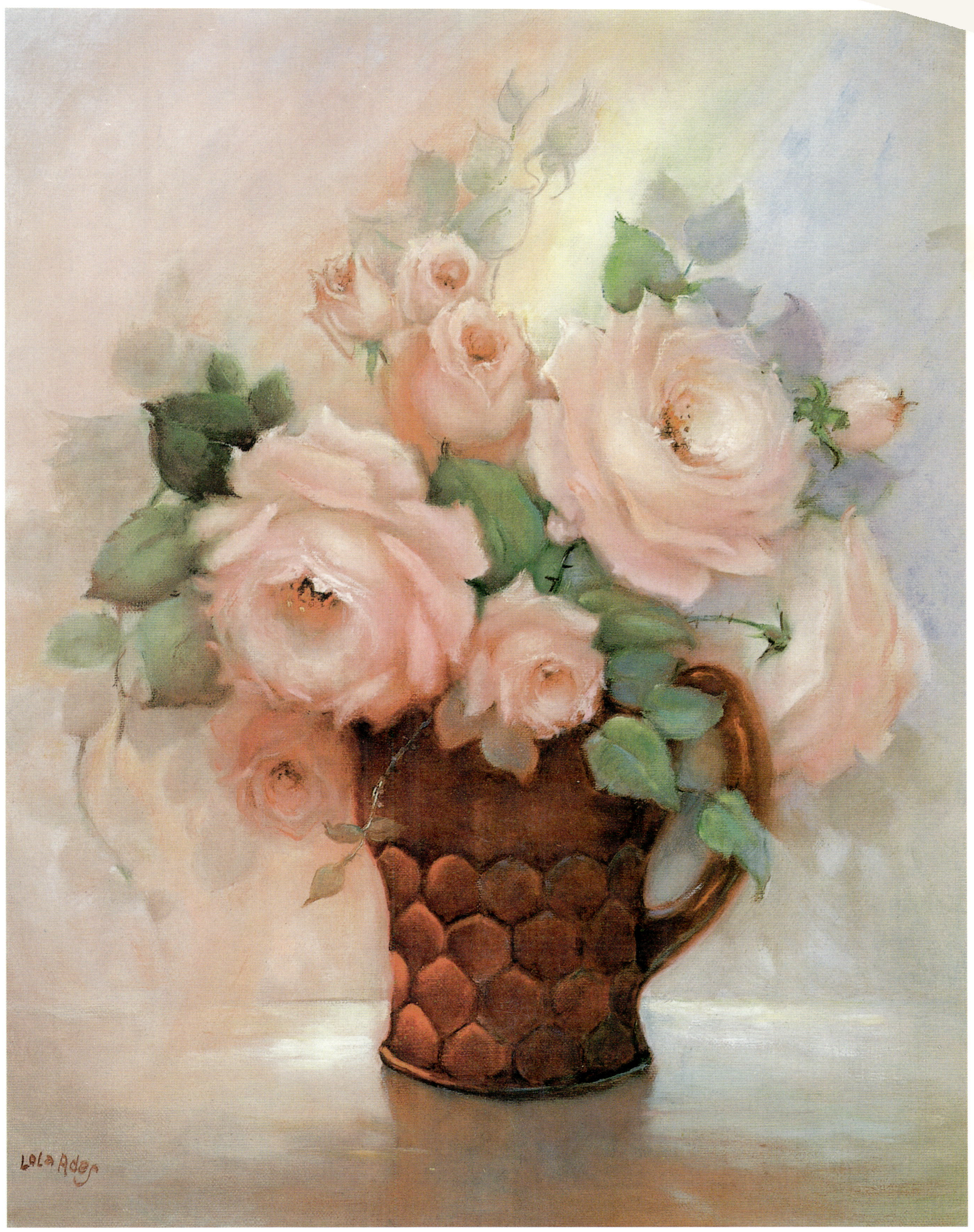

Finish your painting by adding highlights; mix white into the various base colors to create tints, and use pure white sparingly. The light source is coming from the top left, so the strongest highlights are in its direct path. The area at top left is also warmer than the other parts of the painting. In the background, use a warmer, red tint at the upper left, blending it into a soft yellow at the center, and finally transitioning into a cool, shadowy blue at the right. You don't want the background to be so colorful or detailed that it overwhelms your subject, nor do you want it to be so bland that it takes away from the overall impact of the piece!

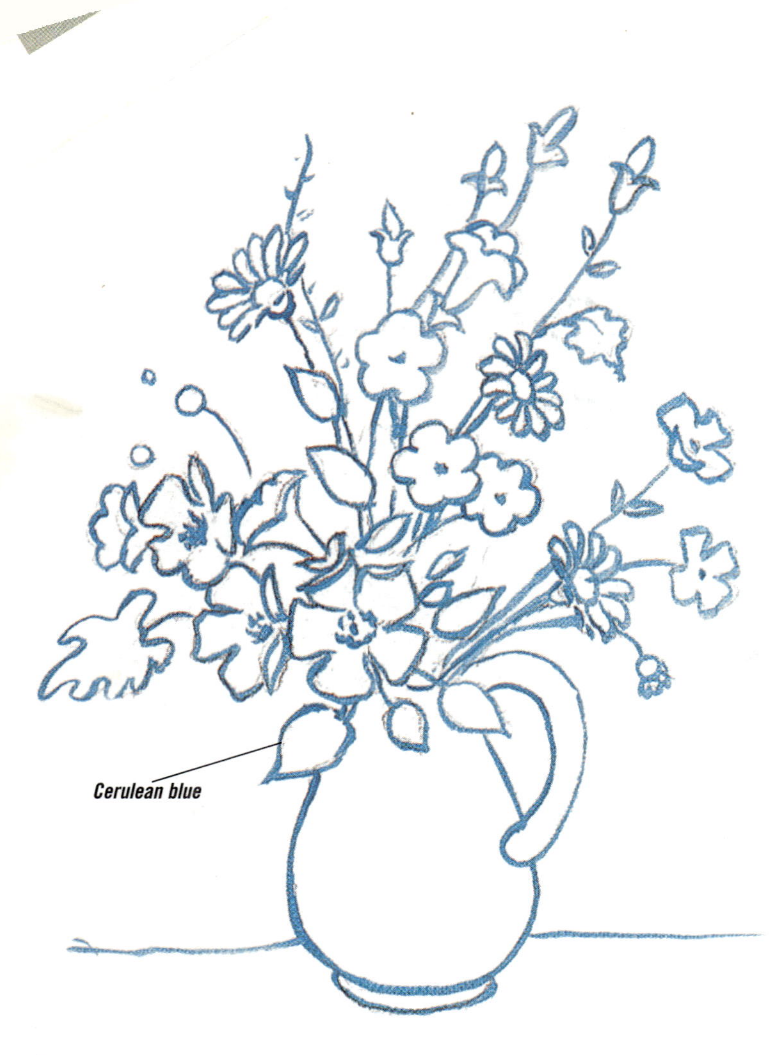

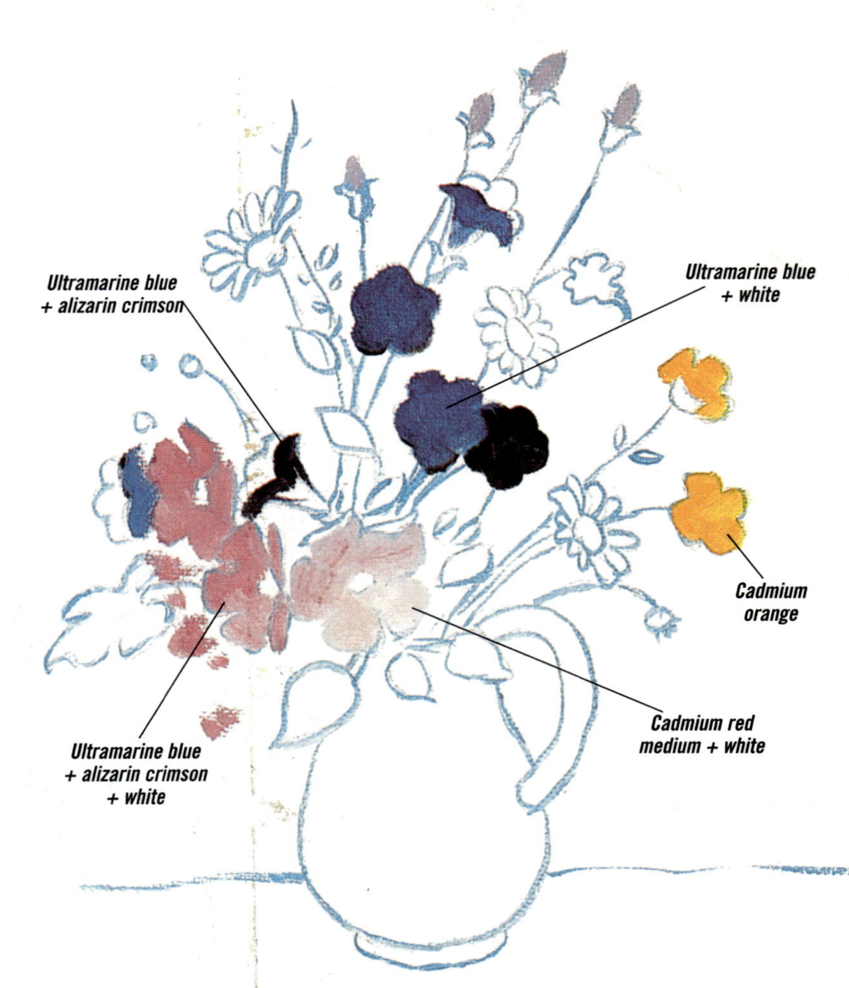

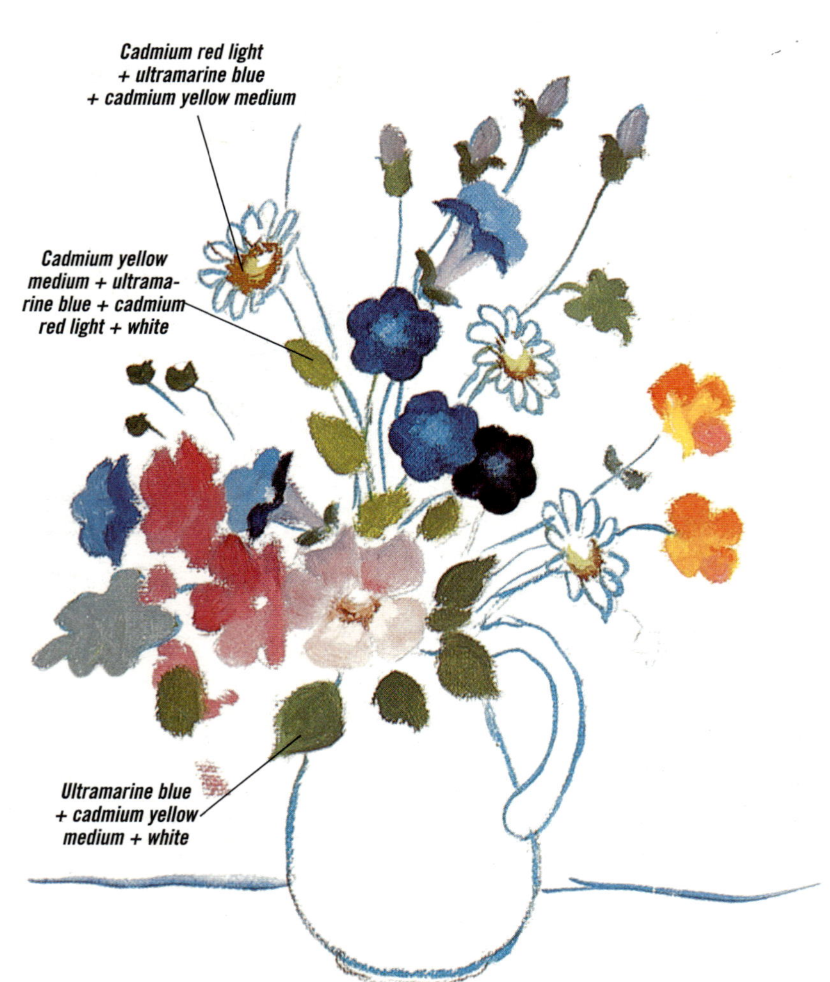

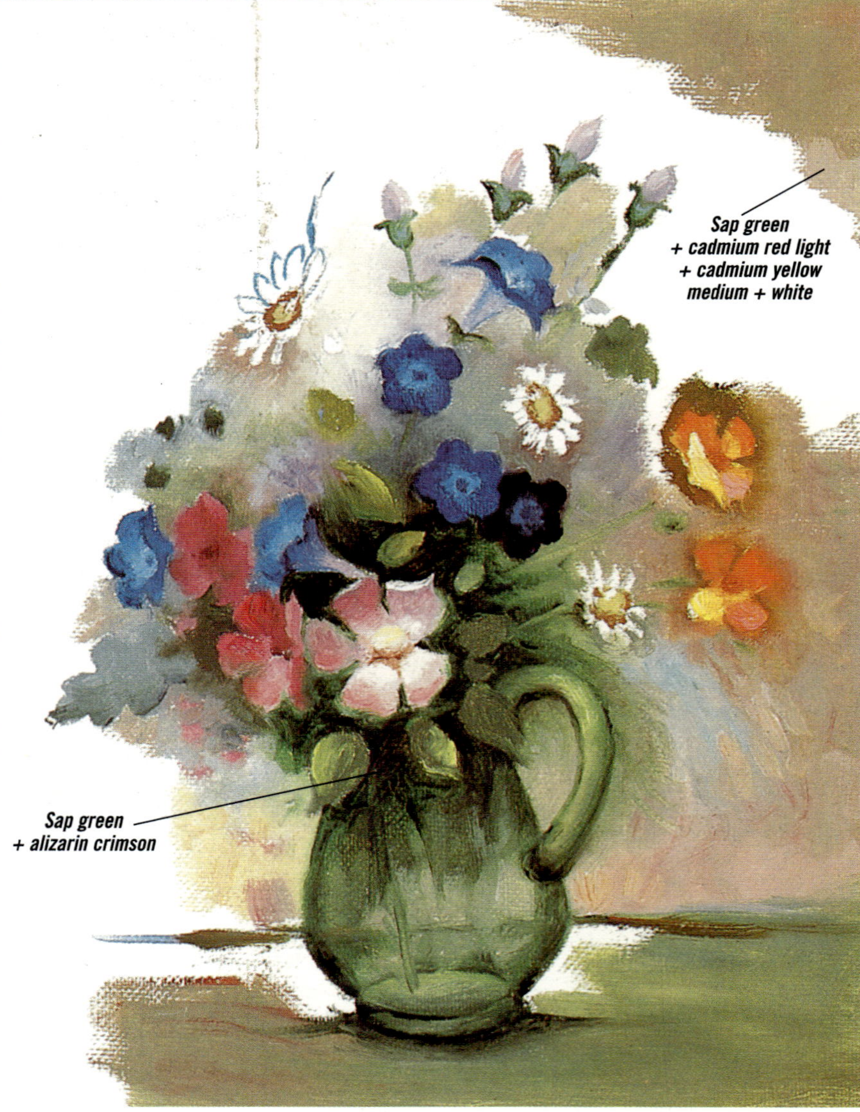

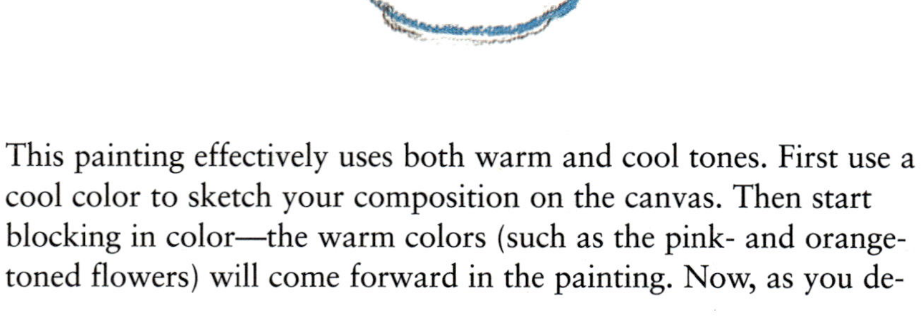

This painting effectively uses both warm and cool tones. First use a cool color to sketch your composition on the canvas. Then start blocking in color—the warm colors (such as the pink- and orange-toned flowers) will come forward in the painting. Now, as you develop your flowers, include both warm and cool tones on the same blossoms. Begin blocking in the background before painting the glass vase with a thin, transparent green. Paint around the petals and the light-colored marguerites.

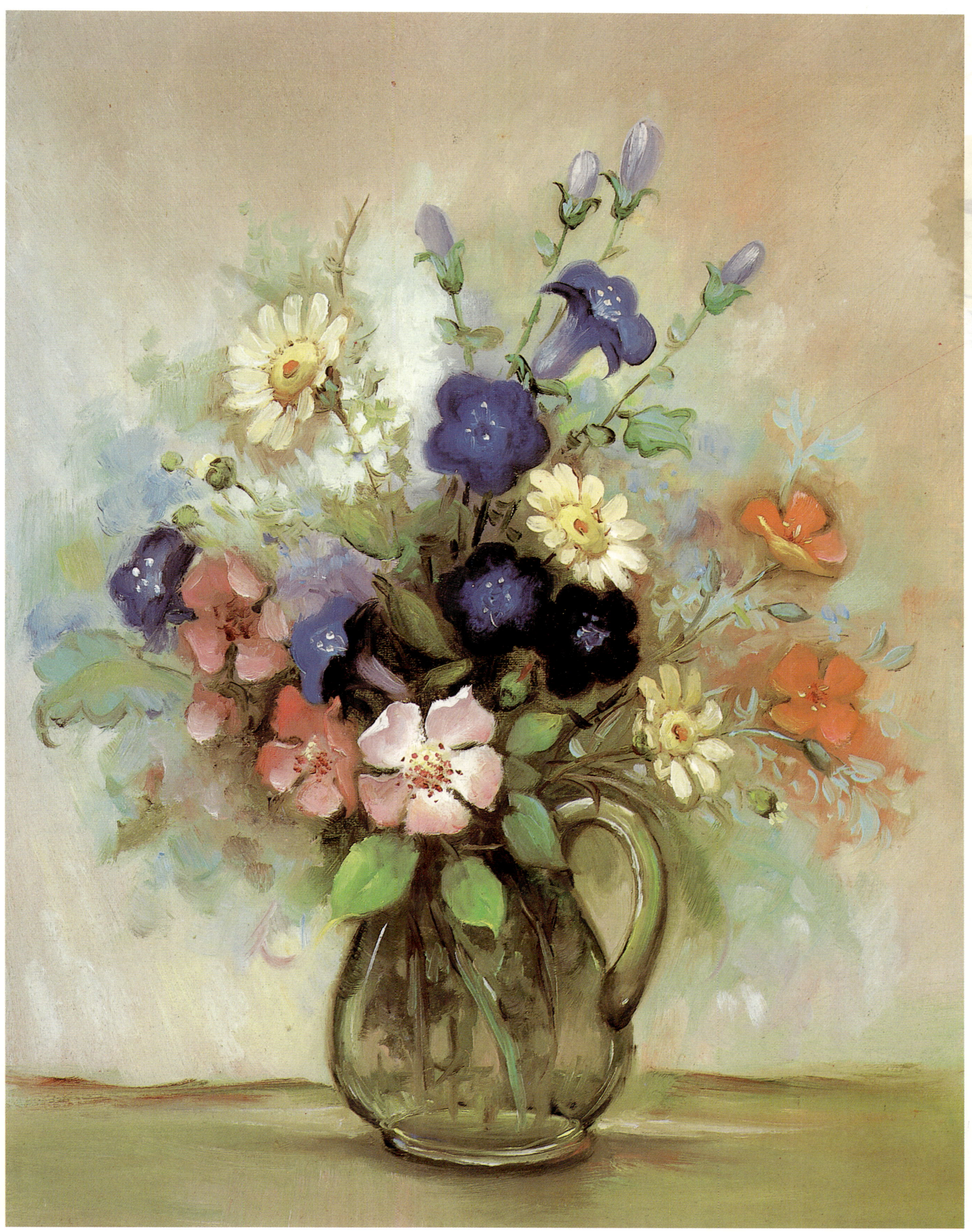

Next paint the suggestion of light, cool-toned leaves in the background, which will cause the warmer and darker flowers to "pop" forward. After the background color is complete, let it dry before painting the light-colored flowers and accents. Paint the marguerite petals with a creamy mixture of white with a speck of cadmium yellow medium. Then add the finishing touches to all the flowers. And don't forget to add the little details, including the colorful flower centers and the highlights on the glass vase.

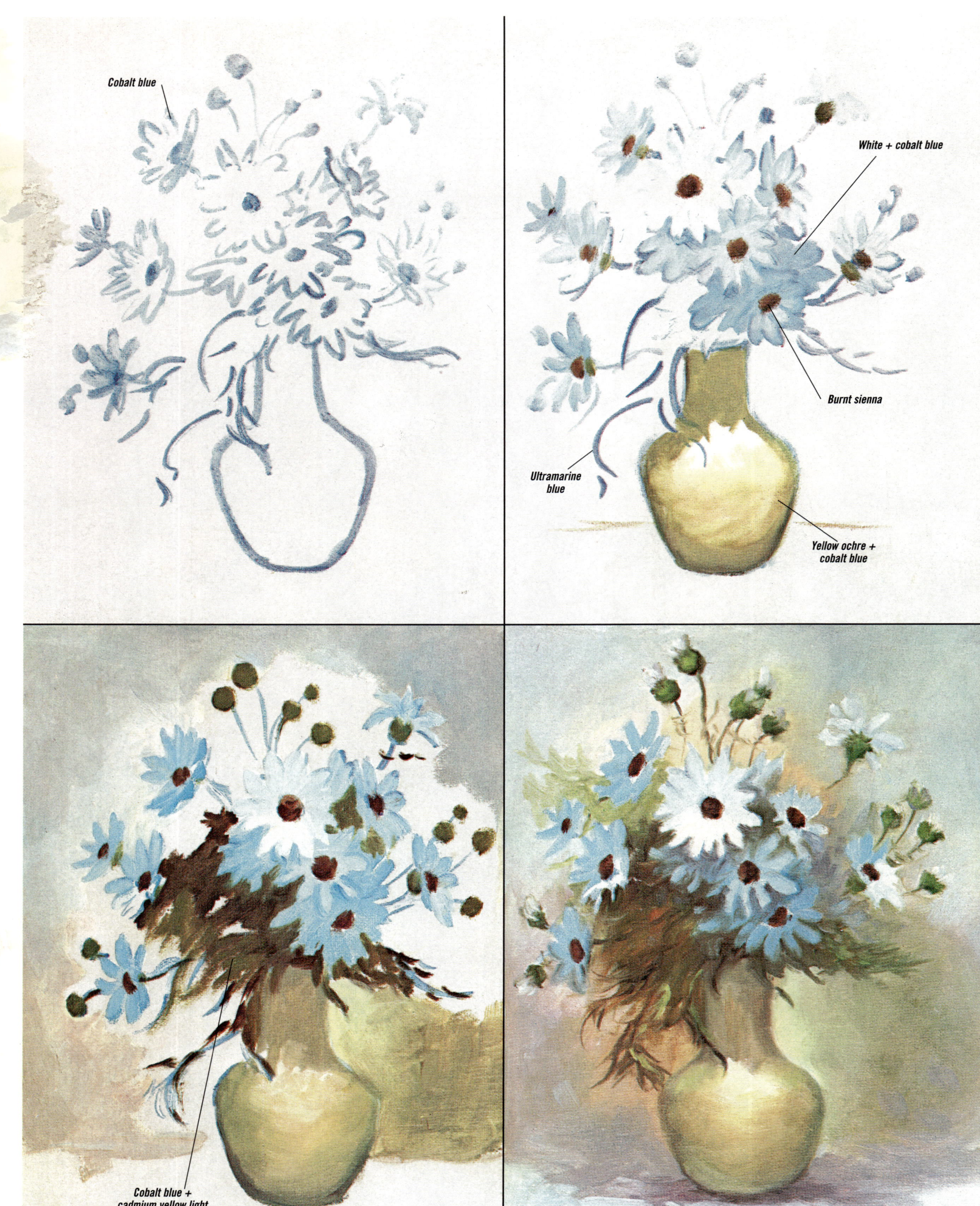

When you paint white subjects, remember that only the brightest highlights are truly white. The remainder of the color contains nuances of the surrounding shades. Start this painting by sketching the basic composition. Then establish the shadowed portions of the daisies and their dark centers, and fill in the darker portions of the base color for the vase. Next paint the dark leaves and buds, and begin blocking in the background. Then refine the background, adding purple shadows underneath the vase and warmer colors behind the leaves at left. The vase is highly reflective, so add hints of other colors from the painting on its surface.

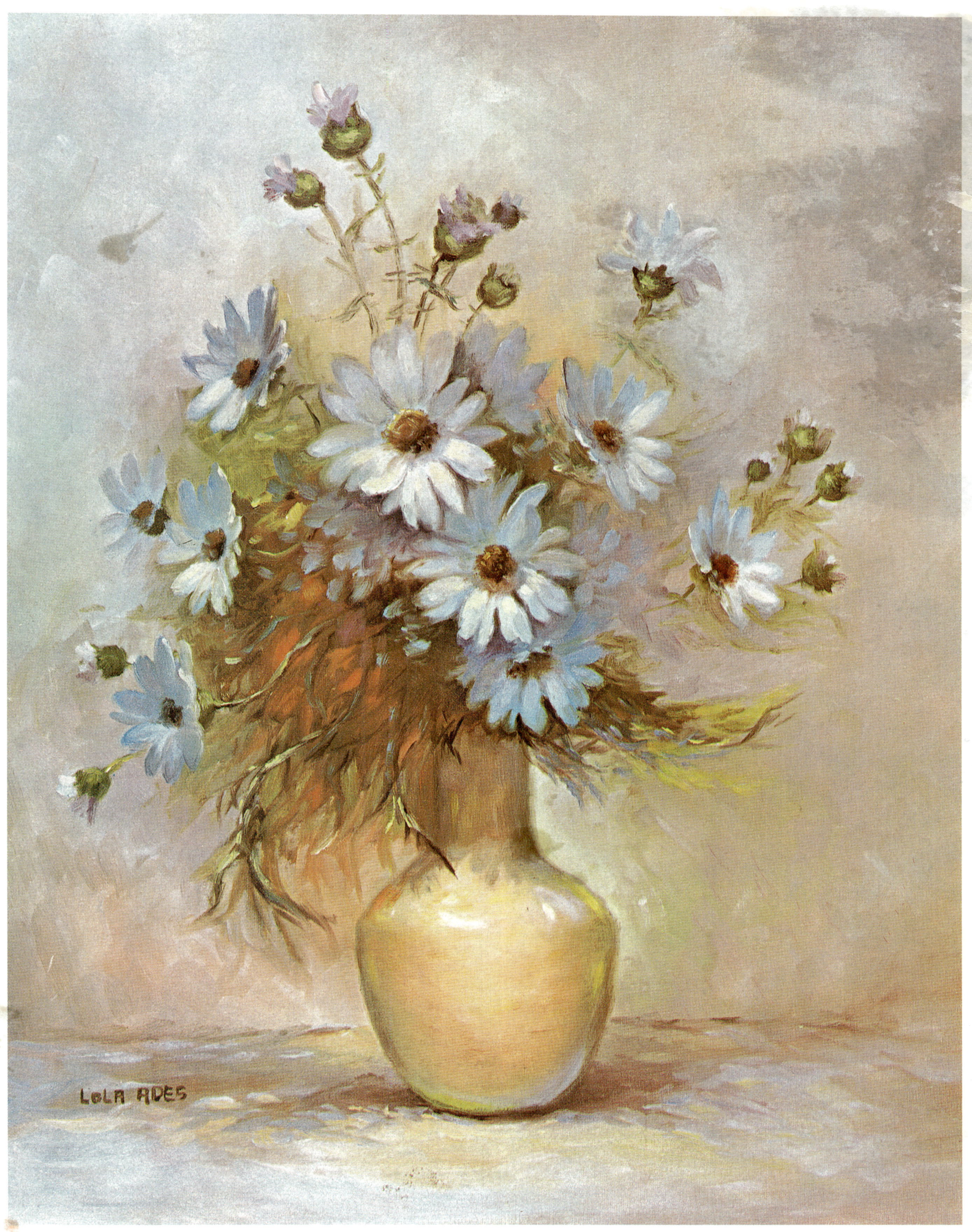

The background of this daisy painting is, for the most part, more muted and neutral in tone than the center of interest; but even within this neutral background, there are areas of more vibrant colors. Notice that the orange behind the greenery creates a dramatic contrast to the cool blue and white flowers. For final touches on the vase, add highlights using cadmium orange and cadmium yellow light. Also use cadmium yellow light to highlight the lightest portion of the leaves, bringing a warm glow to the spots that are touched by the bright light. Add a few darker background strokes to suggest the tabletop, and the painting's complete!

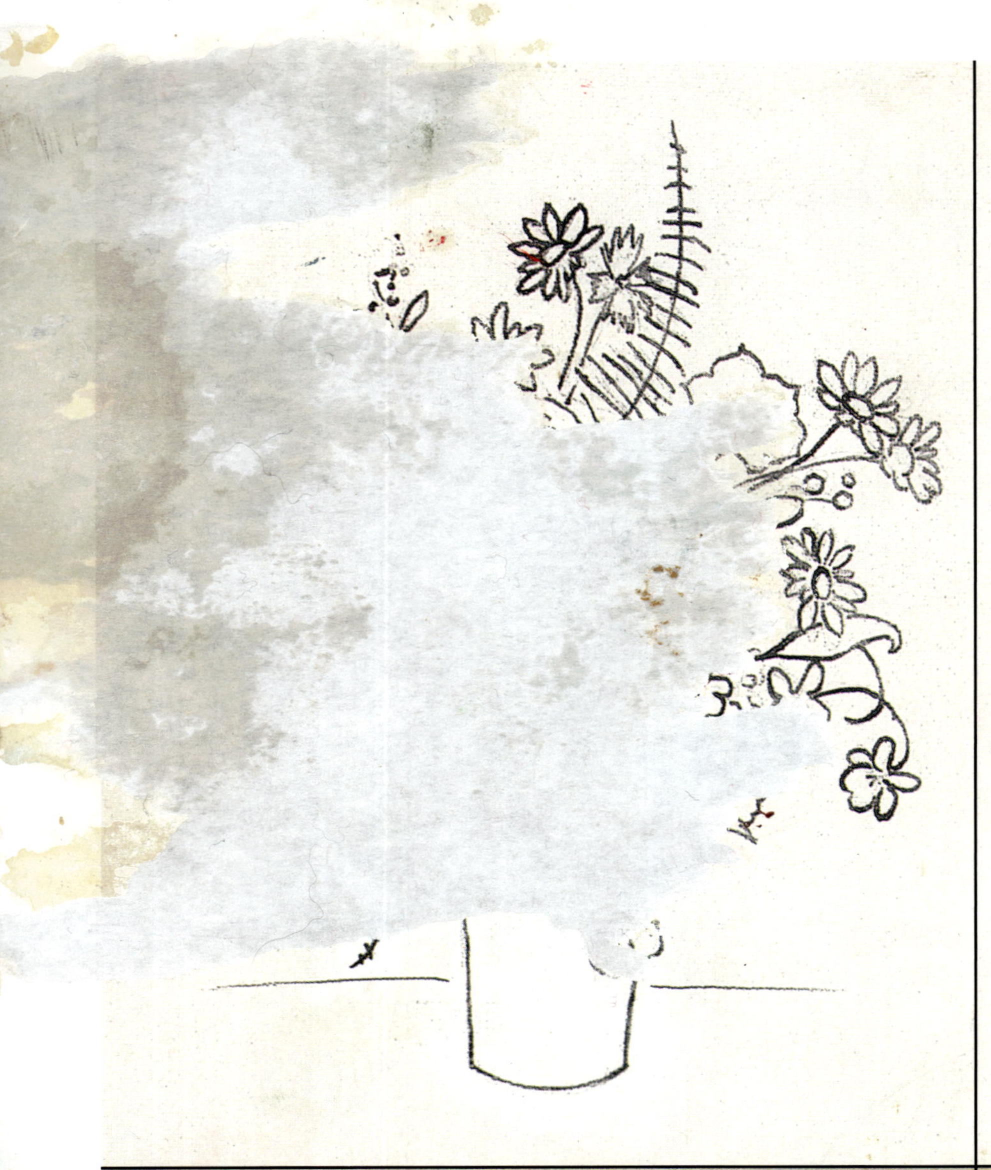

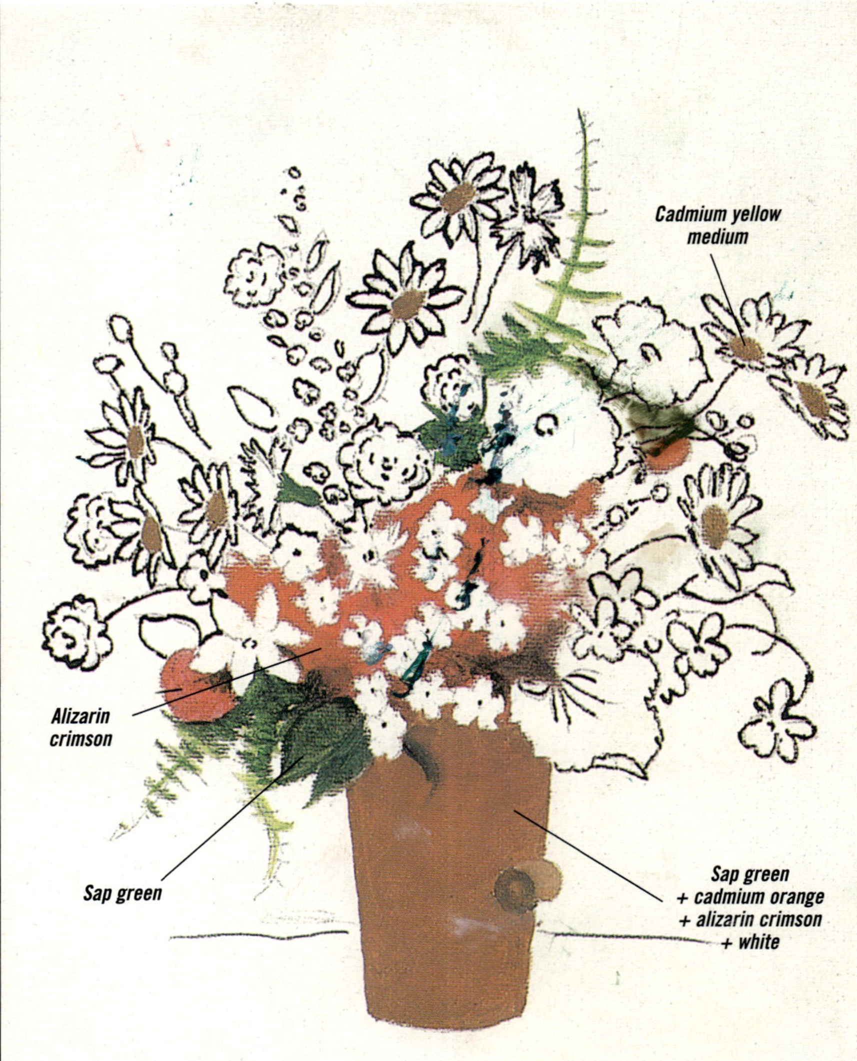

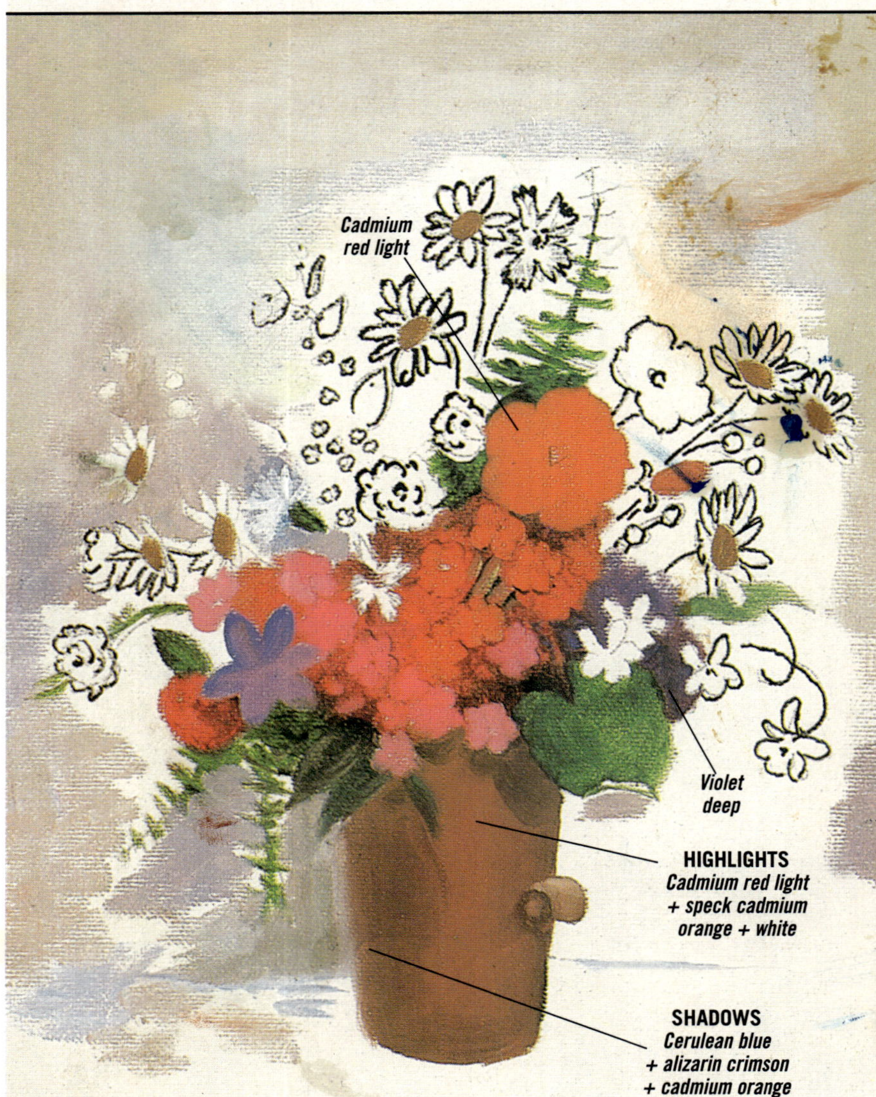

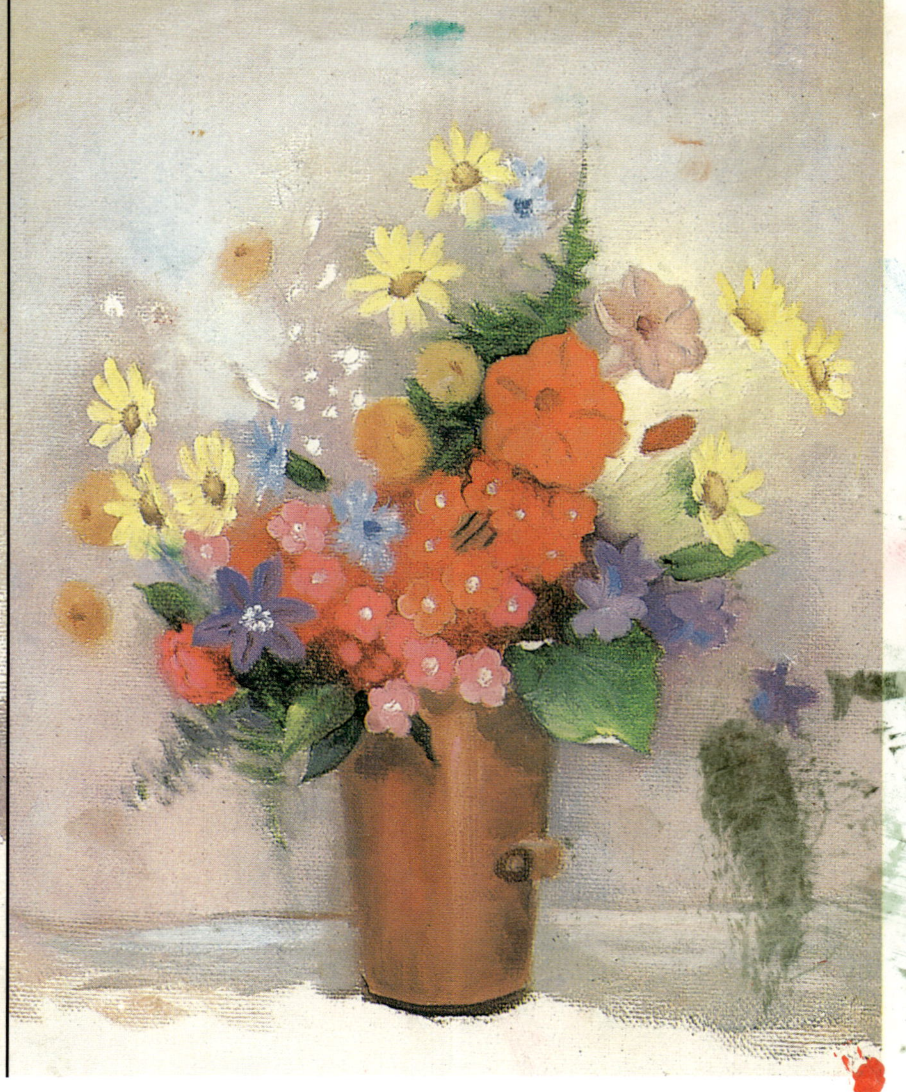

The subtleties of this painting—cooler shades and less detailed accents—call attention to the warm, summery elements. Start your painting with a basic sketch. When your composition is established, begin blocking in the dark leaves, red flowers, and metal container. Even in the dark areas, be sure your color mixes are warm and not too muted. Next start blocking in the background, and add a few highlights and shadows to the copper container. Continue developing the warm flowers at front, and then refine the details. As you paint the various colored accent flowers, add plenty of white to your mixes to tint them and keep the colors soft.

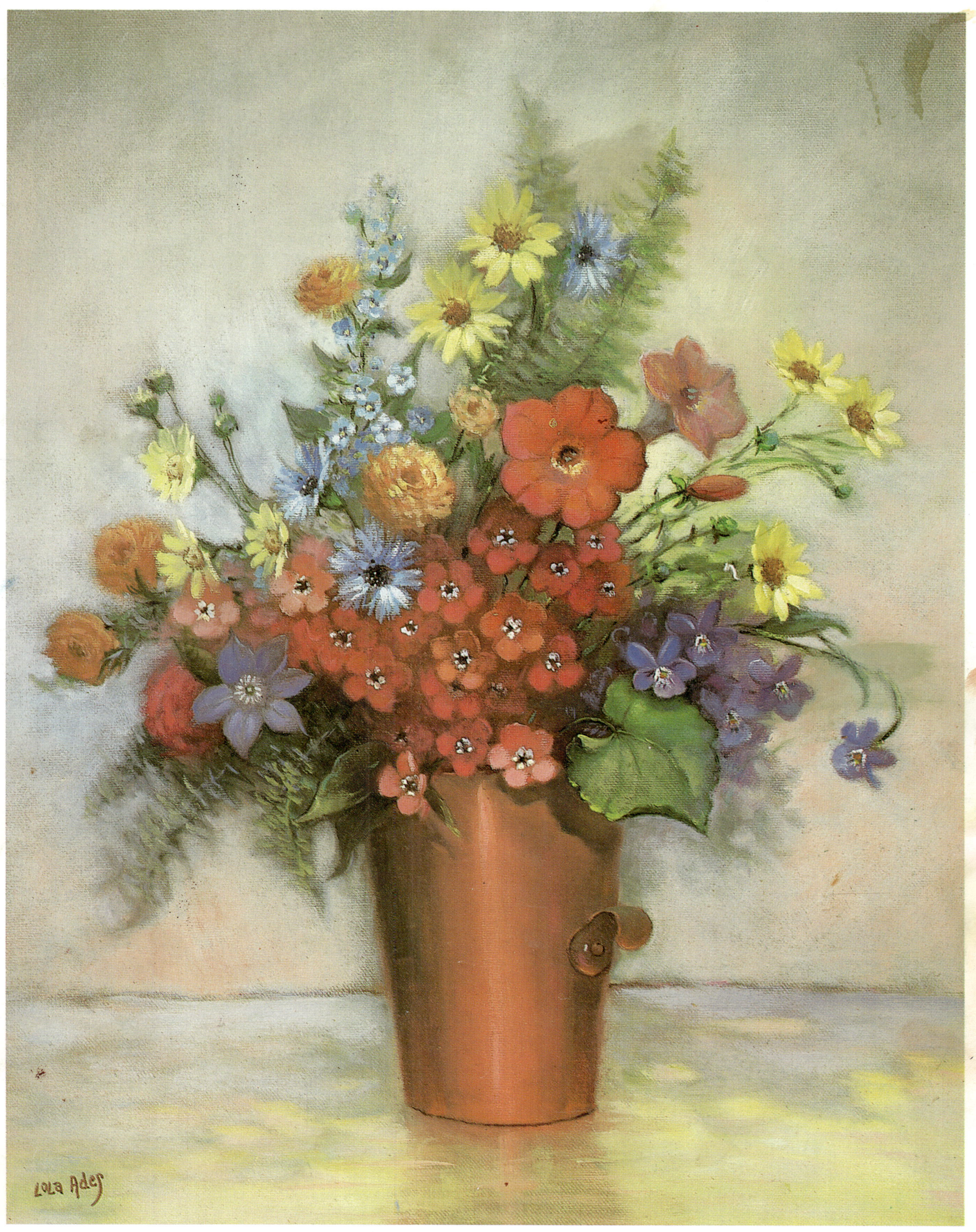

Now finish the background, adding plenty of warm, sunny highlights in the foreground. Then, after the background has dried, paint the small blue flowers and add the final details to the painting. Even the darkest areas of the painting should still maintain the warm tone of the piece, including the dark centers of the flowers. Rather than using a black paint straight from the tube for these areas, try mixing your own to create a less stark, more organic color. You can mix complementary colors together for especially dynamic neutrals. (See page 4.) In this case, red and green are natural choices because they harmonize with the rest of the painting.

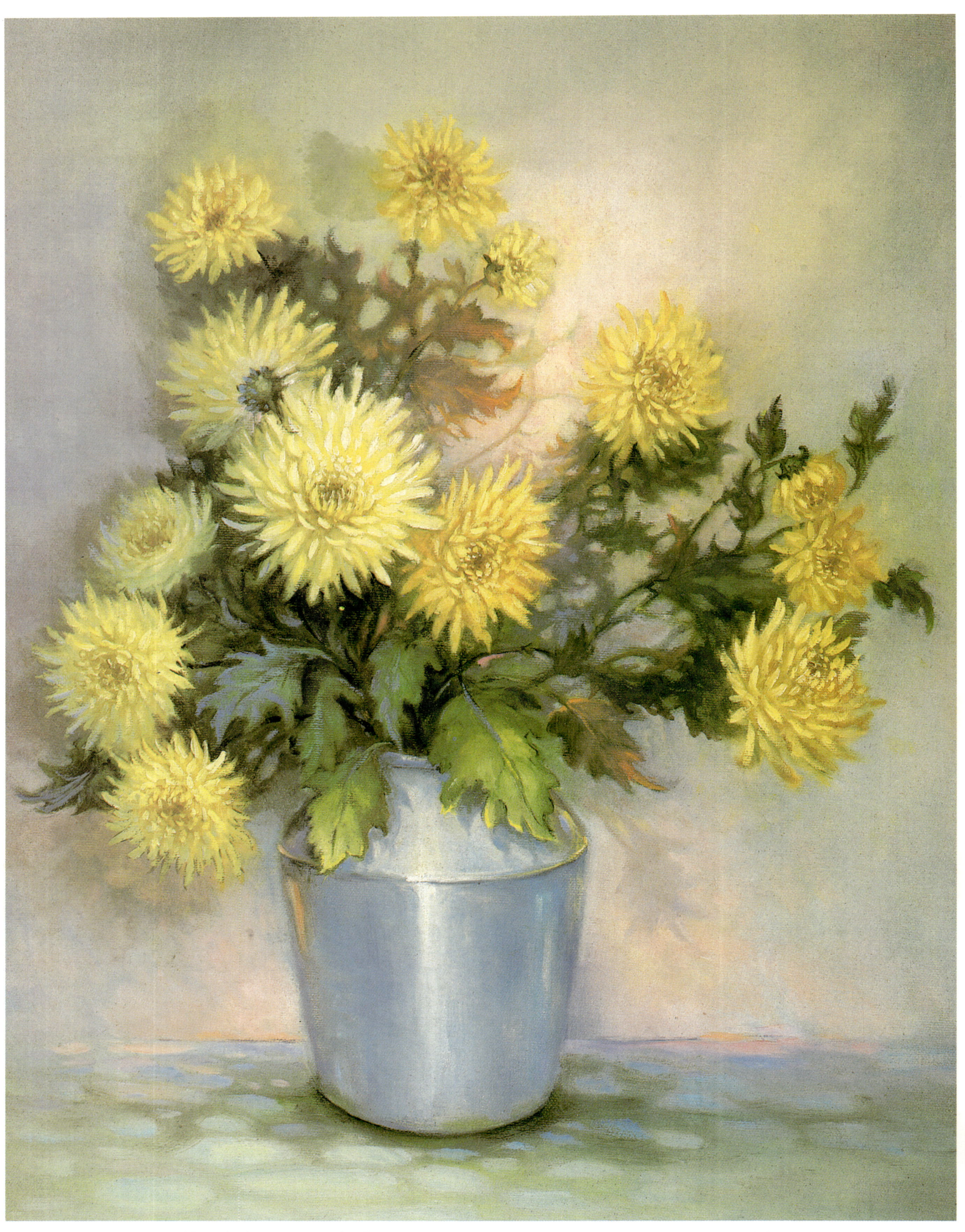

USING ASYMMETRY Although this painting of yellow mums contains only one kind of flower, a plain vase, and a simple background, it is still particularly pleasing to the eye. The variety—and interest—comes from the asymmetrical design. The slight imbalance of this composition makes it more dynamic, and the unexpected departure from the ordinary engages the eye.

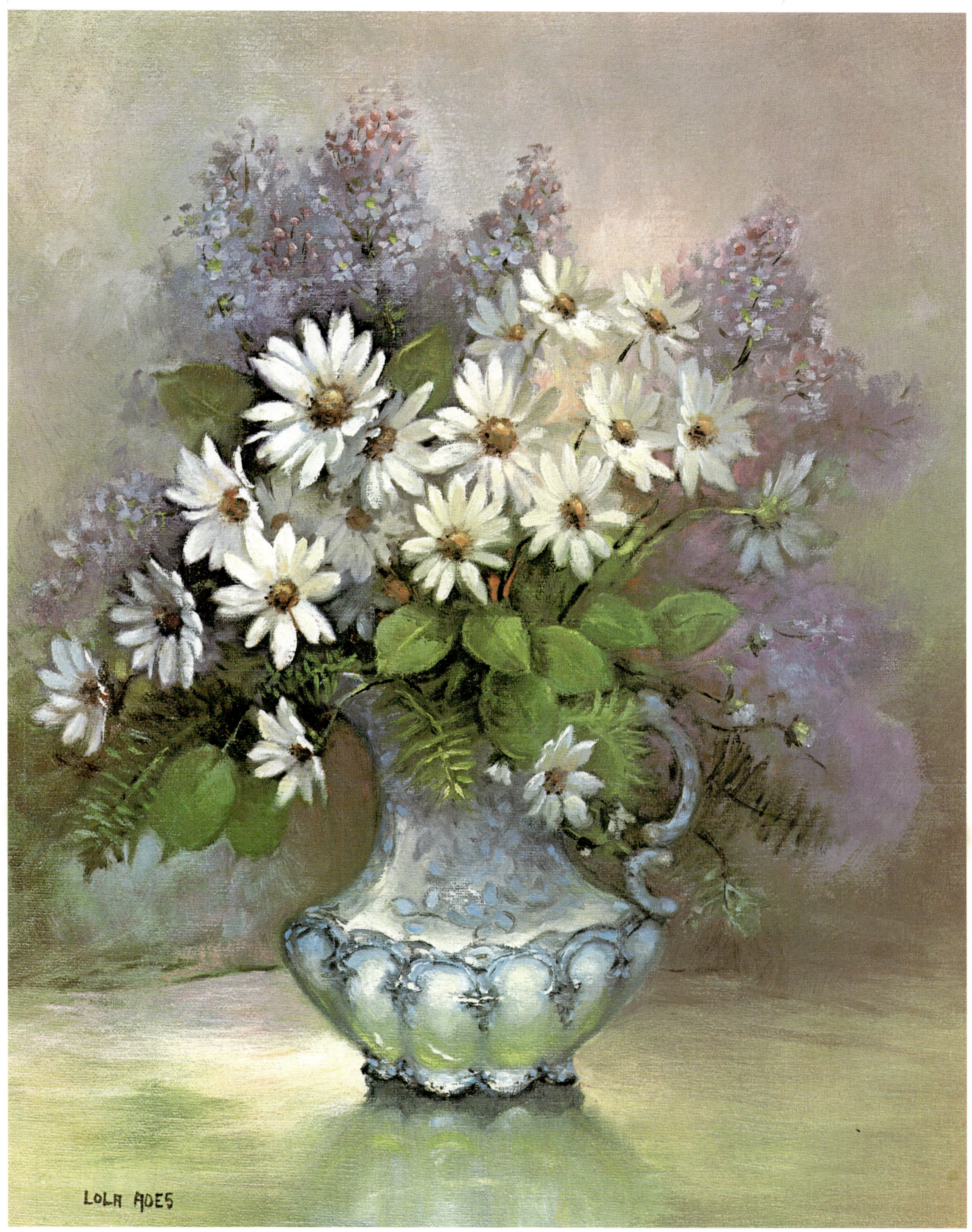

REPLICATING PATTERNS Don't shy away from intricate or detailed objects in your still life compositions. These decorations don't need to be rendered explicitly; paint only the suggestion of detail, and the viewer's eye will fill in the rest. For this elegant vase, both the embossed design and the painted pattern are only roughly indicated in strokes of blues and white highlights.

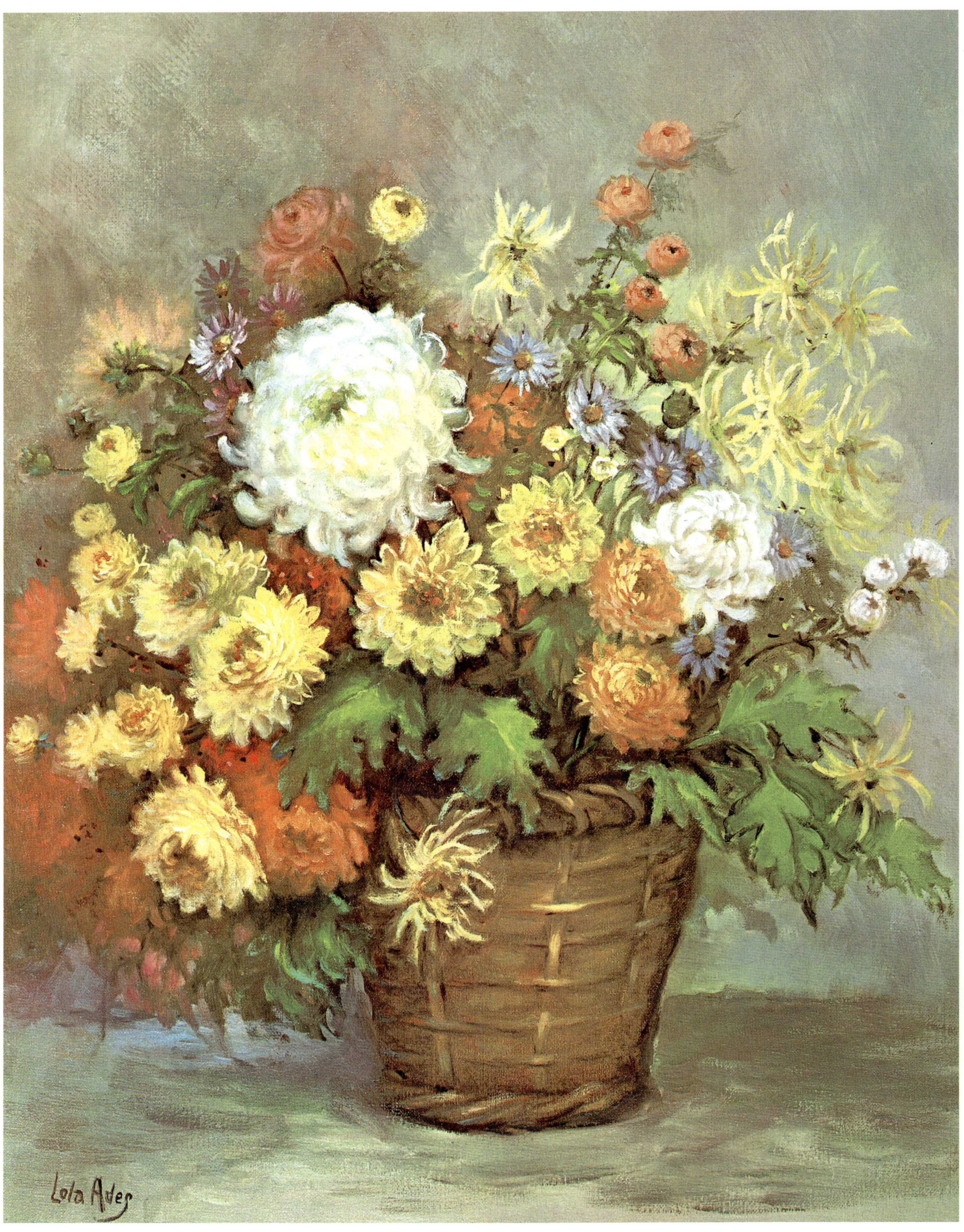

SHOWCASING WHITE Warm-colored flowers typically come forward in a composition, but in this lively painting it's the large white mum that really draws attention. The viewer's eye is automatically attracted to whatever is different in a painting, so including a white blossom amid a colorful floral bouquet is a sure way to create a compelling composition.

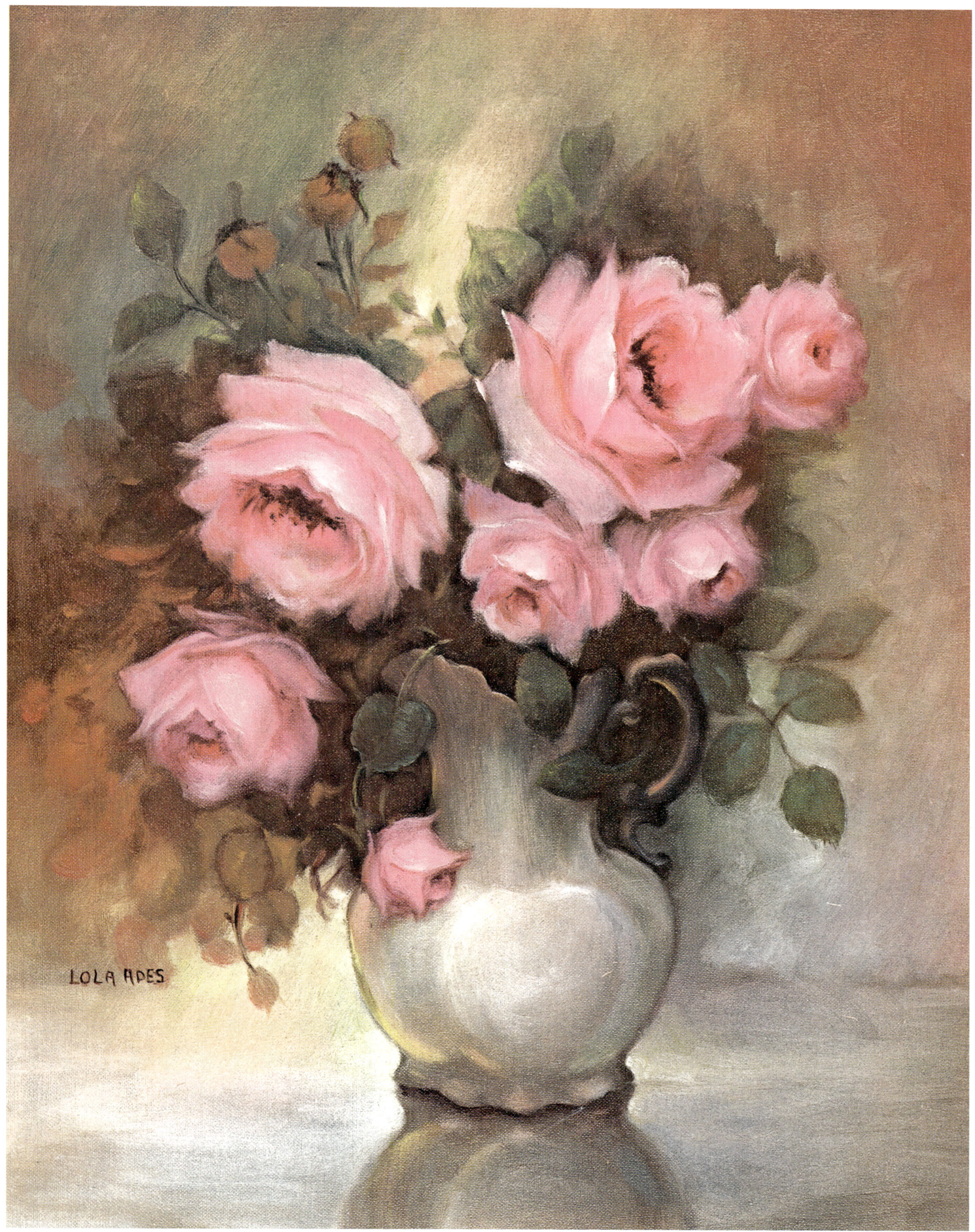

PAINTING REFLECTIONS Another way to enhance a composition is to place your vase on a reflective surface, such as a highly polished or glass-topped table. This creates a mirror image of the vase reflected in the table, as shown here. Although the reflection should imitate the shape of the vase exactly, use slightly darker versions of the colors. And don't forget to duplicate the highlights!

Walter Foster Art Instruction Program

THREE EASY STEPS TO LEARNING ART

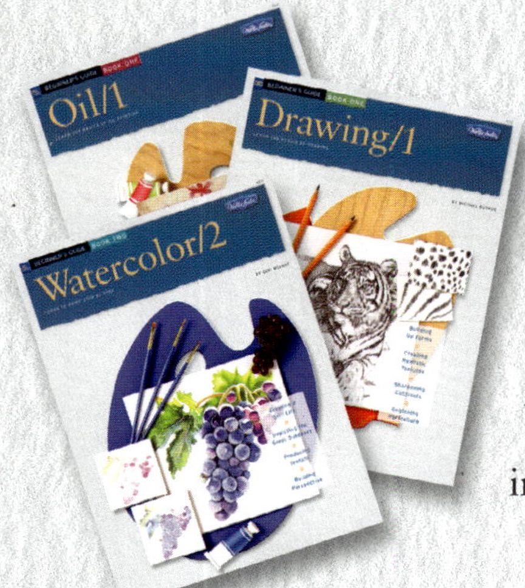

Beginner's Guides are specially written to encourage and motivate aspiring artists. This series introduces the various painting and drawing media—acrylic, oil, pastel, pencil, and watercolor—making it the perfect starting point for beginners. Book One introduces the medium, showing some of its diverse possibilities through beautiful rendered examples and simple explanations, and Book Two instructs with a set of engaging art lessons that follow an easy step-by-step approach.

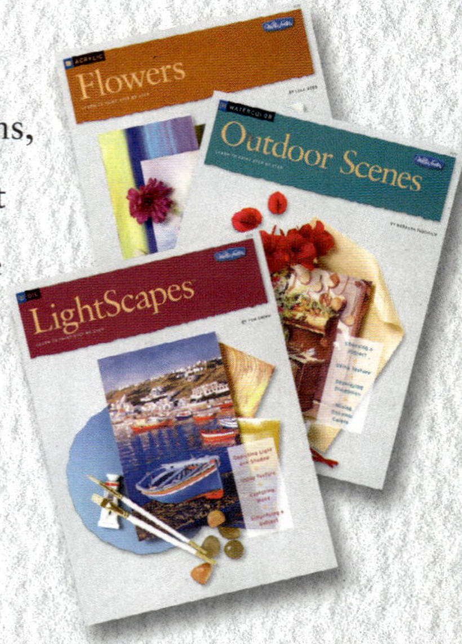

How to Draw and Paint titles contain progressive visual demonstrations, expert advice, and simple written explanations that assist novice artists through the next stages of learning. In this series, professional artists tap into their experience to walk the reader through the artistic process step by step, from preparation work and preliminary sketches to special techniques and final details. Organized by medium, these books provide insight into an array of subjects.

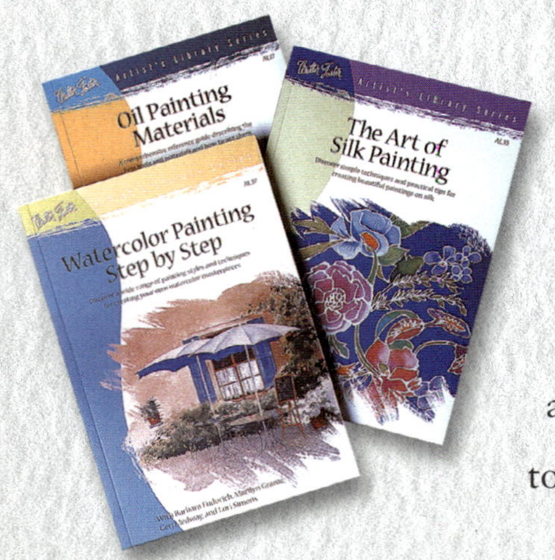

Artist's Library titles offer both beginning and advanced artists the opportunity to expand their creativity, conquer technical obstacles, and explore new media. Written and illustrated by professional artists, the books in this series are ideal for anyone aspiring to reach a new level of expertise. They'll serve as useful tools that artists of all skill levels can refer to again and again.

Walter Foster products are available at art and craft stores everywhere.
Write or call for a FREE catalog that includes all of Walter Foster's titles,
or visit our website at www.walterfoster.com.

WALTER FOSTER PUBLISHING, INC.
23062 La Cadena Drive
Laguna Hills, California 92653
Main Line 949/380-7510
Toll Free 800/426-0099

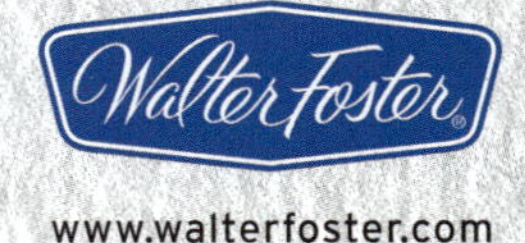

www.walterfoster.com